PRINTS

OF A

PRIEST

Writings by Father Elstan

Fr. Elstan Coghill ꝰ

"We rejoice and give thanks because man --
although he has much in common with the world in which he lives --
at the same time bears the signs of a superior being:
that is, the signs of his likeness to God himself."
– *Pope John Paul II*

PRINTS

OF A

PRIEST

Writings by Father Elstan

COMPILED FROM THE VICTORIA GAZETTE
1985-1996
VICTORIA, MINNESOTA

PRINTS OF A PRIEST
Writings by Father Elstan

Published in the United States of America by
Susan M. Orsen
Post Office Box 387
Victoria, Minnesota 55386
Books may be ordered from the above address.

Susan M. Orsen, Editor.

Library of Congress Catalog Card Number: 96-68734
ISBN 0-9652263-0-1

Acknowledgments

Thank you, Crow River Press in Hutchinson, Minnesota, for your printing assistance -- especially Brian Bleil and Mark Theis.

Thank you, family members of mine and Joan Smith of Wayzata, Minnesota, for helping reformat Father's columns from the *Gazette*.

Thank you, Kathy Kraemer, Marlene Speltz, Sonja Huber, Jesse Coghill, Father Bernardine Hahn, OFM, and Mom and Dad, for keeping with me the secret of this project and knowing with me some of my concerns.

Thank you, Jenny Orsen, daughter of mine who shares with me enthusiasm for this book -- and for life.

Thank you, Nick Orsen, son of mine who smiles at me -- even when I'm not trying to be funny.

Thank you, Allan Orsen, husband of mine, for your steadying influence and love.

Thank you, people of Victoria and other readers of the *Gazette* who continually offer words of support and encouragement.

Thank you, Father Elstan, for being part of my life.

Thank you, Jesus, for life.

Editor Sue

Table of Contents

Introduction

PRINTS OF A PRIEST is a collection of columns written for *The Victoria Gazette* by Father Elstan Coghill during his eleven years as our parish priest at the St. Victoria Catholic Church in Victoria, Minnesota. This book evolved as Father Elstan's retirement from St. Victoria, and full time parish work, was looming. I wanted to present him with a surprise gift, a special gift, a gift unlike all others -- much like the dear Father Elstan.

The Victoria Gazette, my monthly newspaper, features regular columnists who write about subjects of local, and not so local, interest. One columnist in particular has universal appeal, as evidenced by numerous letters to the editor from all over the country that refer to the humorous and entertaining stories of one Father Elstan Coghill, the Franciscan priest who has graced the Victoria community since the summer of 1985.

Father seldom writes directly about himself. From his writings, however, we glean much about him. We learn he is a storyteller who generates and communicates life through his masterful command of the English language. He sees the humor in the sport of life and how God may have winked when he created us. He accepts -- and loves -- people as they are, yet cajoles us to be more like Jesus. He is a happy priest, who swings from the branches of the tree of life, enjoying the fruit along the way, never upsetting the balance of nature, but enhancing it in playful and unpretentious fashion. He is a character, a one of a kind, a bright and funny man. And, yes, he is holy and humble.

As I read and reread Father's work in preparing this publication, I was reinforced in my conviction that it has remained, over time, fresh, humorous, and instructive on the nature of humankind. His writings are, in my estimation, timeless. Some will have you laughing out loud. Some you will be reading to friends. Give yourself time to get to his best stories. Many of them are miniature masterpieces and worthy of being preserved for posterity. Hence, this compilation.

May his writings brighten your days, as they have mine and those of countless other people. I think you'll enjoy the turn of phrase, the wit and wisdom of Father Elstan Coghill.

-- Sue Orsen, Editor

"The steps of a man
are from the Lord,
and He protects him
in whose way He delights."
–Psalms 37:23

A Roller Coaster of Events

by Father Elstan
August 1985

I was welcomed to Victoria with a flurry of events -- some sad, some happy.

Frieda (er, that's my puppy) and I moved into the rectory on June 19th around noon, about an hour after Father Agnellus departed for Nebraska. By bed time I was exhausted. So was Frieda. The next day I had to go back to Chanhassen for a luncheon date with Father Barry; the secretary of St. Hubert Church, Ev Wagner; and the housekeeper at St. Hubert rectory, Joyce Horr.

The day after that I had to go back to Chanhassen for the wedding rehearsal of a young man I had received into the church some time before, Fred Lien, and the daughter of Joyce Horr. I had committed myself to their wedding long before I was transferred.

The next day the wedding took place at about the same time that Mark Giesen and Lisa Flygare were being married here at St. "V's." Thank God for Father Robert Schmieg who stood in for me here. He is home from his mission in Brazil and has been a big help to me in these first few confusing days -- helping me to get acquainted and helping out when needed.

On Sunday, June 23rd, we celebrated the Golden Wedding of John and Gertrude Schmieg at the 10:30 Mass.

The next Sunday was another happy event. Bishop Ham came to officially install me as pastor of St. Victoria Parish at the 10:30 Mass. The reception in the Parish Center after the Mass was a delightful follow-up for the bishop, the people, and me.

A sad event on Monday, the 24th, we buried William Mitchell.

Then a happy event. Father Matthias Kiemen and his sister spent a day with me. Father Matt is an old professor of mine from my seminary days.

Another happy event on Saturday, June 29th, the wedding of John Trebesch and Monica Leuthner. But a sad event followed on Friday, July 5th, when we buried Elizabeth Zanger.

Then Sunday, July 7th, an old buddy of mine (since 1936), Father Flavius, drove in from Columbus, Nebraska, the town where Father Agnellus is presently stationed, and spent some time of his vacation with me.

Then a downward swing of emotions. May (Mary) Boll, the mother of our Bede Boll, was buried at St. Boni on the 10th of July.

And there have been meetings. I would classify them as happy events: the meeting with the Catholic Aid Society, the session with the Board of Education, the parish council meeting, the delightful luncheon with the senior citizens and the 4H groups at the Town Hall, and the joyful celebrations at 8 a.m. with the from 40 to 60 people who gather every morning for Mass.

It has been a roller coaster of events and emotions, and a full and interesting month -- my first month at St. "V's."

I appreciate this means of keeping in touch with you through the *Gazette*. More next month.

Moments of High Drama

by Father Elstan
September 1985

There were moments of high drama at St. V's this month.

Of special note was the day early in the month when Mrs. Wartman was sprucing up the Parish Center and took some garbage out to the area boxed off for that purpose and discovered a black cat with white sergeant stripes running the full length of his body and down his tail, helping himself to some breakfast.

Julianne Wartman is no fool. She sensed the problem immediately, called the marines, the national guard, and the fire department, and the fire department responded. One of the men tossed a smoke bomb into the garbage area and "Stinker Katt" headed for the woods in high indignation, pausing just long enough before he disappeared to give the gathered spectators a very nasty look. Thanks for the help, men.

It was also exciting to watch the two hot air balloons get inflated and launched from our ball field. It looks like a fun thing to do.

Then, on Sunday, the 18th, a happy group of server boys and chaperones left the parking lot of the church for the metrodome to watch the Twins do battle with the Mariners. For an awful moment in the first inning it appeared as if the Twins might spoil their record, but by the end of the game, they managed to lose again, 7 to 2. The boys and I are grateful to Mr. and Mrs. John Heiland who arranged the happy day for us, and to the people who drove and chaperoned. Jay Schmieg captured a foul ball and refuses to divide it with his brother and sisters.

The carpet in the Parish Center hasn't been cleaned since the day it was installed. Thanks to Bonnie Fritz who arranged to have it "done."

We had a beautiful wedding on the 23rd -- Marlin Tony Sackett and Roxanne Notermann. God bless your marriage, Marlin and Roxanne.

A lot of things happening next month. We'll tell you about it in the next *Gazette*.

Some Things on Hold

by Father Elstan
October 1985

Some things at St. V's are still on hold. The tree stump along the road is trimmed and waiting for the sculptor. I can't tell you how long that wait will be, but it is best to leave the wood dry and cure for a while before the work is begun. We are talking about the statue of St. Victoria that we want carved in the tree stump.

Also waiting is the work on the expansion of the parish office area, although that will probably be underway by the time this report goes to press. We'll have more to say about the progress of the work in next month's *Gazette*.

Something that couldn't wait was the work of cleaning up the sacristy. Not once Mrs. Jendro got her crew together and turned them loose. I'm glad I had to be gone that day for a clergy meeting, or I might have been trampled to death.

Our CCD (Confraternity of Christian Doctrine) program started with a meeting of the two coordinators with the volunteer staff of teachers, and Sister Jane Hurly from the Catholic Education Center. If that kind of spirit lasts the whole year, it will be a great year.

And people are still getting married. Bruce Moore and Jean Lundquist said, "I do," on September 21st, and Mike Kreklow and Marcia Meyer said the same thing on the 28th.

Babies were born and then reborn since you last read the *Gazette*. At St. V's they were John Francis Gregory, Reilly Jay Schoo, and Sara Rose Wessbecker.

More in due time.

+++

P.S. The old fence between the cemetery and the woods has been removed and we celebrated the 65th (that's not a misprint), the 65th wedding anniversary of John and Ruth Konschak this month at a 10:30 Sunday Mass,

Some Inconvenience

by Father Elstan
November 1985

Last month's St. Victoria Church News started with the sentence, "Some things at St. V's are still on hold." This month's news could very well start out with the same words.

The statue of St. Victoria that we intend to have carved in the tree stump on the edge of the road just south of the church has not been carved yet. Some time ago I invited the ladies of the parish to volunteer to pose as a model for the statue. No one has come forth yet. Maybe that's what's holding things up.

But one thing that is well under way is the work on the expansion of the office. The new space will be approximately 330 square feet -- an improvement of about 230 square feet over the old area. We are paying for the anticipated luxury in terms of present inconvenience. Much of the office equipment had to be moved into the living room. As a result, the living room isn't very livable. Frieda got lost in the litter and confusion the other day and she didn't surface for five hours.

The inconvenience has been felt by the parishioners too. There is no doorbell operating. The front door has been blocked off periodically. The yard is muddy and the church and sacristy are dusty, but all have taken it in high good humor. Perhaps by the time the next issue of the *Gazette* reaches you, I can have an invitation in it to you to come and see the finished product.

The annual Catholic Aid Society's rummage sale at St. Victoria on October 3rd and 4th was well organized, well stocked, and well patronized. As a result, it was most successful.

Preparations are already under way for the Mission Carnival to be held during Lent. The ladies are gathering twice a month to sew for the event.

The grade and high school students from St. Victoria had a perfect day for their hay ride on the 16th.

Ray and Frances Schmieg mowed the cemetery this week, probably for the last time until next spring.

James Robert Heiland, John and Joyce's son, joined the church through baptism since you last read the *Gazette*.

The St. Victoria unit of the Council of Catholic Women had a most interesting meeting on the 15th, when they had as their speaker, Mr. Fay Elliot, the state racing commissioner.

And I think that's all for now folks.

Saint Victoria the Martyr

by Father Elstan
December 1985

In the church's calendar the Feast of St. Victoria is celebrated on December 23rd.

I don't know if our church was given the name of St. Victoria because of the name of the town -- or the town was called Victoria because of the name of the church. Whatever the case, I thought you might be interested in reading what is known about St. Victoria, as contained in *Butler's Lives of The Saints*.

"The record of the sufferings of St. Anatolia relates that when she refused (because of a vision) to accept her suitor, Aurelius, he went to her sister, Victoria, and asked her to persuade Anatolia to marry him.

"Victoria's efforts were not only unsuccessful, but she herself was converted to her sister's views and broke off her own betrothal with one Eugenius.

"The young men then removed the maidens from Rome to their respective country villas and tried to starve them into a different frame of mind. Anatolia was denounced as a Christian, and her end is thus summarized in the Roman Martyrology on July 9th.

"After she had healed many throughout the Province of Picenum who were suffering from various diseases and had brought them to believe in Christ, she was afflicted with several punishments by order of the Judge Faustinian, and after she had been freed from a serpent that was set upon her and had converted the executioner Audax to the faith, lifting up her hands in prayer, she was pierced with a sword.

"Victoria met with a similar fate, perhaps at Tribulanon in the Sabine Hills. She refused either to marry Eugenius or to sacrifice and, after working many miracles whereby numerous maidens were gathered to God, she was smitten to the heart by the executioner's sword at the request of her betrothed.

"Both St. Anatolia and St. Victoria had a cultus in various parts of Italy, but the real circumstances of the martyrdom are not known. The sentiments regarding marriage expressed in their record of sufferings are of the exaggerated and unguarded kind which, though often found in Christian documents, approximate more to the heretical doctrines of Encratism than to the teaching of the Catholic Church."

A blessed Christmas to all from the St. Victoria Catholic Church.

Maude Arrives

by Father Elstan
January 1986

Events of staggering proportions filled the month of December at St. Victoria's Church.

Great progress was made on the expanded office project. All that is left to complete is the wall covering and the window drapes. I think in next month's report I will be able to invite you in to see the "finished article." I think the people of St. V's can be proud for having provided this lovely facility.

And then there's "Maude." She entered the life of St. V's on December 15th. Some friends in Chanhassen invited me to a Christmas party on that date. When they were opening some gifts they brought out this animated handful of silk -- a miniature dachshund. She's short of stature, but long in suspension; short on manners, but long on vitality. Frieda is trying to teach her the former and curb the latter.

I've called her Maude because there seems to be a certain incongruity between that name and that puppy -- like calling Kareem Abdul Jabar, "Shorty," or Telly Savalas, "Curly."

Christmas at St. V's was merry in all aspects -- with one notable exception. Some time between 1:30 p.m. and 8 p.m. a thief or thieves got into the house and into the safe and purloined the currency and coin from the Christmas collection. I can't help but wonder what my guard dogs were doing during this activity. To the unhappy criminal(s) I would like to point out -- YOU MISSED $8.43 of my penny ante money that was right under your crooked nose(s) -- and may a diarrhetic bird of paradise hover over your head until restitution is made.

Watch this column for further developments in the progress of the new office, the lives of Frieda and Maude, and the result of our prayers to St. Dismas, the good thief.

Blessing on the Thief

by Father Elstan
February 1986

Since I last wrote to you, every detail of the new parish office complex has been completed except for the window drapes -- and one piece of furniture. Give us another couple of weeks and then stop in to see the finished product.

What you will see, in addition to a beautiful office, is an accumulation of livestock. Besides Frieda and Maude (my two guard dogs), there are 783 birds, representing many species, right outside the office window, and a variety of fish in a large aquarium placed against the back wall. If any more critters congregate here we will have to apply for a license to operate a zoo.

And it may be of interest to you to know that the curse placed on the party or parties who purloined a portion of our Christmas collection didn't work. (I believe the accepted description of the guilty one would be "alleged thief.")

Anyway, the money hasn't been returned yet. Nor has the insurance company compensated us either yet, come to think of it. Maybe a blessing would help. "May the bird of paradise alluded to in last month's column have bad aim at least occasionally."

One of the parish sages, upon being informed about the incident, was heard to remark, "I certainly hope the money was taken by some good, honest person."

I had a pleasant trip to and from Chicago the week of the 19th of January, to take part in a seminar study-discussion for and by the Franciscan Pastors of the Sacred Heart Province. The location was our retreat house at Oakbrook. Some 55 men attended.

The retreat house is on the same land as our old minor seminary, which is now being transformed into expensive housing units. A number of us got a tour through one of the units which is complete and on display. After the tour we all felt like we are living in abject poverty.

Not all the time was spent in serious pursuits. In two evening sessions I won $6.83 playing penny-ante poker. Father Brendan and Father Simon were there, also the Bishop of Saganaw. The Pope didn't make it, however. I hope to be a better pastor of the flock because of this experience.

Saints and Sinners

by Father Elstan
March 1986

The 3rd of February was the feast of St. Blase. St. Blase is the patron saint whose aid is invoked against ailments of the throat. Traditionally, after the Masses on the weekend closest to that date, the congregation is invited to come to the front of the church and receive individually the blessing of the throat.

The formula is several lines long. Virtually everybody in the congregation responded to the invitation. By the time I had given the last blessing to the last person after the last Mass on Sunday. I had a sore throat.

A few days after this, Lent began with the same people approaching the altar to receive the blessed ashes as a reminder of their mortality. There was a book written in the '50's called *Saints with Dirty Faces*. As folks walked out of church after Mass with ash smudges on their foreheads, I thought of that book, even though it had nothing to do with Ash Wednesday, nor could all those who received the ashes be classified as saints.

On the 16th of February the Victoria branch of the Council of Catholic Women held their annual mother-daughter breakfast. Bonnie Fritz, the president of our council, invited Mama D to speak at the occasion. You've heard of Mama D. She has a restaurant that bears her name in Minneapolis. She shows up on TV occasionally. She speaks to any group that invites her, and brings her unique message, bubbly style, and Latin personality to bear most effectively. She kept the large audience here at St. Victoria listening, thinking, smiling, and sometimes laughing for the duration of her talk.

In the course of her talk to us she told us the story of how one time for some occasion at her restaurant, she needed a statue of St. Anthony. The priest who had arranged for her to pick it up at the church was not there when she went for it, and the one who was there didn't know about the arrangement, and wouldn't let her have it -- so she stole it. I sneaked out of the breakfast a little early and came over to the church and nailed down all the statues.

And the Catholic Aid Society had their annual breakfast on the 23rd. They tell me it was the largest crowd ever to attend here, and I can believe it. If the numbers had been any larger, we would have had to eat our breakfast in the parking lot.

I hope the crowd at our approaching Mission Carnival on March 9th will be equally as impressive. It will be all right with me if the numbers are so large we run out of everything except money.

The Angel was No Guardian

by Father Elstan
April 1986

Notable among events that have transpired over the past month is the completion of the carving of the St. Victoria statue. If you are cruising down St. Victoria Drive and you see a large "lady in wood" in front of the church, don't lose control of your car. It's the finished product of Mr. Barry Pinske rendered in the stump of a dead elm. That's one way of putting life into a defunct tree.

Also of gripping interest to you will be the report that the fish in my tank developed the bad habit of dying for no apparent reason. I hardly thought they were drowning, and they couldn't all be that up in years. One day I was netting a deceased angel fish out of my tank when I bumped a statue of St. Francis that had been submerged for decorative purposes. (I had two statues, one of the Guardian Angel and one of St. Francis, that seemed to be the perfect decoration in an aquarium.) The statue began to disintegrate. Both statues had been contaminating the water for some time. The statues made beautiful decorations -- but lethal.

And notable among events that will transpire is a visit to St. Victoria Church on April 5th and 6th by Dr. Elizabeth Holland. She will talk after the 5 p.m. Mass on April 5th (so 5:45 p.m.), and after the 8 a.m. Mass on Sunday, April 6th (so 8:45 a.m.), and after the 10:30 a.m. Mass on Sunday, April 6th (so 11:15 a.m.), in the church.

Her subject is: "The Victims of Pornography." Her presentation will take about an hour, but it won't seem that long. Her talk, I can assure you, will be gripping and motivating. It will also be explicit and graphic. It is advised that only adults attend. Her video cassette on the subject is considered the most powerful anti-pornography visual presentation in America today, but she will be here in person.

She knows whereof she speaks. Dr. Holland is a Memphis pediatrician, past chair of the Memphis/Shelby County Child Abuse Committee, and has served as chairman of pediatrics at St. Joseph Hospital in Memphis. She shares her story about victims of pornography she has treated. Hope to see you there.

Oh, say, have a glorious Easter.

Preview of Coming Attractions

by Father Elstan
May 1986

More on the wood sculpture of St. Victoria in front of our church...
The Catholic Bulletin (the diocesan weekly newspaper) sent a man out from St. Paul who got some photographs of it, along with a brief story on how it came about. The man promised it would appear within the next few weeks. When it does, I hope their office is prepared to handle the flood of new subscriptions that will be the inevitable result of that feature.

A preview of coming attractions: At the evening Mass on May 10th, a parish mission will start, to continue till Thursday evening. It will be presented to us by Fathers Michael and Carson Champlin. They are blood brothers and members of the Dominican order, the order of preachers. And preachers is just what they are -- of the highest quality.

I heard them about two and a half years ago at St. Hubert's. I went to their first presentation -- just to hear what they sounded like -- and then came back for every one of their talks after that. You will, too, I think, if you come for the first session. I would like to extend the invitation to attend to all of the *Gazette's* vast reading audience, whether Catholic or not. Their theme will be "Spirituality for the '80's and Beyond."

Did you ever hear of the program called "Renew"? You probably will, off and on over the next couple of years -- occasionally in this column. The Archdiocese of St. Paul and Minneapolis is urging every parish in its jurisdiction to adopt this program designed to reach every member of the parish, active and otherwise, to bring about a renewed spirit of prayer, learning, unity, and a lot of other good things.

St. Victoria is committed to the program. The organizational work is presently in progress, and the more it goes on, the more enthusiasm is engendered. I look forward to St. V's becoming, in this decade, a community of saints and scholars.

There is a pair of squirrels in the maple tree outside of my office window. If I could catch them, I would baptize them "Mr. and Mrs. Moamar Kadafy." They haven't actually perpetrated any terroristic acts, but they have spread a great deal of terror among the birds who inhabit that tree.

It was good talking to you.

A Prize for the Pastor;
A Jolt for the Enemy

by Father Elstan
June 1986

You probably won't believe this, but give it a try.

At the beginning of the school year last fall, Marge Leuthner talked me into investing sixty of the parish dollars in twelve raffle tickets. The raffle takes place once a month at Guardian Angels in Chaska. The purpose of the raffle is to help G.A. finance the school. I am presently $440 ahead of their game -- as my name was drawn for 1st prize last month, and 1st prize is $500 worth of groceries at any Super Valu Store.

Let me hasten to add, the above narrative does not describe a totally unmixed blessing. Few blessings in this vale of tears are. Formerly, I garnered a harvest of sympathy from letting it be known that I had never had any luck in bingo, lotteries, the Irish sweepstakes, *Reader's Digest* drawings, raffles, and very little in poker.

That whole line is now ruined. The sympathy will no longer be forthcoming. Some of us are called upon to bear excessively heavy crosses in this life.

The old devil took a nasty beating at St. Victoria's on May 4th when our second grade class received their Lord for the first time ever. If you need some potent prayers, get one of those little angelic creatures on your case.

And the above-mentioned old enemy is in for another jolt on the 29th of this month when the freshmen members of our St. V's family will be possessed by the Holy Spirit by the imposition of his hands and the anointing by Bishop William Bullock. Congrats, class! Sorry, Satan!

The parish was treated from May 11th to the 16th to the powerful, personal, and personable treatment of the subject, "Spirituality for the '80's and Beyond," by our two friends from the Order of Preachers, Fathers Mike and Carson. Thanks, men, for what you did for our family.

That's all from St. V's at this time, folks. Have a safe summer and a happy one and remember, there is no vacation from the practice of your faith.

"My Tail is Told"

by Father Elstan
July 1986

Say, did you see the article on Barry Pinske, our chain saw artist, in that "other paper" – *The Minneapolis Tribune*?

It is a source of some pride that we, the *Gazette*, scooped "that other paper" by about two months, and it seems will have scooped the diocesan paper by about two years. They, *The Catholic Bulletin*, promised to feature our chain saw sculpture of St. Victoria in their paper, but have not done so yet.

Incidentally, there is a spelling mistake in one word in the inscription at the base of our statue. Did you notice it?

Early this spring Tony Aretz put up three wren houses in various locations around the outside of the rectory. Two couples took advantage of the free housing. I believe the results are all happy ones because I notice serious looks on the faces of the jenny wrens -- and the "old man" wrens have their chests out and are bragging loudly to the local fauna when they aren't checking for bargains in cigars.

If the anticipated population explosion materializes, maybe next year the third house will be occupied. Remember, you saw it first in the *Gazette*. That "other paper" will just have to copy it -- with permission, of course.

I'm recording these events just one day before St. Victoria's will realize a singular honor. Four of our friars of the Sacred Heart Province are being sent to the interior of Alaska by our (their) superiors to work in six villages of Eskimos (Indians).

They chose as their official send off site -- Victoria. Father Provincial, Dixmas Donner, the director of the Franciscan Missionary Union, Father Thomas Vos, plus assorted other friars of the province will be here for the big event.

It's too bad they aren't being sent from here in January. The culture shock would not have been so great. I wonder if these missionaries have heard about the baby polar bear sitting on an iceberg in Alaska who, when asked to tell his story, responded, "My tail is told."

I think I'd better sign off.

Taking a New Approach

by Father Elstan
August 1986

It is probably not too late to report that on the 1st of July I drove over to Guardian Angels and loaded into my car whatever Father Clem hadn't already put in his, in preparation for our trip to Columbus, Nebraska.

Father Clem had been transferred there from Chaska. He was to follow me out to Columbus. The plan worked well till we got to Sioux City. Have you ever tried to wind your way through Sioux City?

The town seems to have been laid out by a demented Ogalalla Indian. Anyway, it happened. We got separated and didn't see each other again for the next 120 miles and 4 hours -- in the backyard at St. Bonaventure's in Columbus.

That reminds me. There is a town in Nebraska by the name of Ogalalla. Two patrol men stopped a car speeding through the town. They were cops with a commendable sense of duty, but a limited ability to spell. The one writing up the ticket turned to the other and asked, "How do you spell Ogalalla?"

The one to whom this conundrum was posed pondered it for a time and then said, "I don't know. Let the guy go and we'll stop him again when he goes through Ord."

While in Columbus I saw your former pastor, Father Agnellus. He sends you all his greetings and wants you to know you are the greatest. He didn't say "greatest what." He looks well and showed no signs of slowing up until we went out to lunch together and the waitress brought the tab.

As you all know, the Second Vatican Council strongly encouraged a "new approach to the church." Accordingly, we are ripping out the old sidewalks and concrete in front of the church here at St. V's in preparation for what will be brand new and wider sidewalks.

At present the area looks like the abomination of desolation spoken of by the prophet Jeremiah, but that will all soon be changed. If you are listening, Father Bernardine, you must know that the sidewalks and entrance to the church that you installed served well the tread of many pious feet for the last thirty years, but it was all beginning to show the signs of wear, weather, and weeds coming up through the cracks. Also, if you are listening, you will recognize the famous quote from the prophet from Jeremiah.

If any of you are interested in my nomination for the best joke program on TV, watch our Minnesota Twins. They've got to be twins. It would take two to be that bad.

Well, folks, that's St. Victoria as of July 21st, 1986.

St. Victoria Church News

from Editor Sue
September 1986

Father Elstan is in Wisconsin somewhere fishing for muskie. He'll be gone for 3 weeks so should have some good stories to tell next month -- as any fisherman would!

St. Victoria is pleased to have Father Donelus serve the parish during the fishing trip. He and Father Elstan were buddies in their earlier years and they still are.

Remember in last month's issue of the *Gazette*, Father Elstan spoke of the Second Vatican Council encouraging a "new approach to the church"? Well, the new approach at St. Victoria is finished. Vogel-Michel Cement out of Victoria did a fine job designing and constructing the new entrance and sidewalks at the church. Their design included an exposed aggregate cross in the middle of the cement entrance to the church. It looks great.

"Miserere" in Wisconsin

by Father Elstan
October 1986

I'm sure the reading public can scarcely wait to get the story of my fishing trip to Wisconsin, so here it is. It falls into the classification of a short story, but a true one.

We (Father Hugo, Father Matt, and I) went up to Lake Cor D'Orielle (I think that's the way it's spelled -- it's pronounced coo-der-aye). We went there because it is ballyhooed as the best muskie lake in Wisconsin, if not the world.

Apparently someone caught a 69-pounder out of that lake in 1952 and they've never forgotten it. If our experience is any basis for judging, that was the last of the line. We didn't even get a "follow."

To make matters worse, one cold rainy day -- after hours of futility -- we were pulling into the dock, and I placed one foot on the dock and still had the other one in the boat when our expert helmsman (for reasons that escape me) threw the motor in reverse. Everybody made a wish as I made like a wishbone.

Now I know why there are no muskie in that lake. That water is so uncomfortable.

To add to my woes, we had to sleep in a dorm arrangement. I'm not used to sleeping in the same room with anyone -- much less one who talks in his sleep. Father Hugo recited the "de profundis," the "miserere," and the prayers at the foot of the altar as clearly as if he had a congregation of 1,000 behind him. The other one had a constant snore that sounded like a hippopotamus in heat.

Anyway, I missed my eight hours of the old dreamless every night I was there, and came home exhausted and feeling so sick that if I'd have felt just a little better, I'd have been able to get up and go to the hospital.

In the ensuing week I recovered enough to take part in "Sign-up Sunday," the occasion when the parishioners indicated their intentions to take part and preferences in taking part in RENEW.

After the excellent response of the people in this event, I felt well enough to fly to Chicago for my annual retreat. The retreat ended Friday morning. My return flight was to leave Midway at 12:50 p.m. I was scheduled to be home for the wedding of Alvaro Gomez and Nancy Bongard at 5 p.m. When I got to the airport, Armageddon broke loose. By the time the rain let up and the lightning subsided, it was a moot question whether I'd be home in time for the wedding. I made it with fifteen minutes to spare, but with my fingernails chewed down to the elbows and my nerves on the raw edge.

I'm glad to be done with September and settle down to the merely hectic.

Mistaken Identity

by Father Elstan
November 1986

Have you ever been in circumstances where you were constantly being mistaken for someone else?

Over the past year and a half, salesmen have stopped in to greet me warmly as "Father Agnellus." "Good to see you 'again,' Father Agnellus." "Father Agnellus, we have this wonderful product you can't afford to be without," etc., etc.

I always tried to correct them before they had mispronounced my name so often they would be embarrassed when the awful truth were made known -- that Father Agnellus and I have very little in common. He's Polish; I'm Caucasian. He's older; I'm young. My name is "Elstan," etc.

What was happening is that they would stop in front of the church and study the sign where Father A's name is still posted. I had two alternatives. I could either have my name officially changed to "Agnellus" or I could have the sign repainted. I chose the latter.

There is need, also, of a sign indicating which is the church side door, the sacristy door, and the office door. Not a few of these enthusiastic salesmen, and others not acquainted with the entrances and exits here, have spent long hours in the cold knocking on the church or sacristy door while I'm sitting in the office unaware of their presence. That problem is being corrected by a sign strategically placed.

The only other event of note in the ongoing historical development of St. Victoria's in the past month occurred when I bought a roll of 200 stamps and left them on my desk when I went to Chaska for supper one night.

During my absence Maude, my dachshund devil, discovered the stamps. When I returned, she was sitting in the middle of the office floor with stamps and pieces of stamps pasted to her nose, her jaws, her tail. It was a super-human effort that prevented me from posting a Melbourne, Australia, address on her fanny and dropping her in the "out of town" slot at the post office. She had plenty of postage adhering to her to get her there.

The Ugliest Christmas Tree

by Father Elstan
December 1986

If you look back at your past Christmases, isn't there one that always stands out in your memory? There is for me a Christmas that I recall with mixed emotions -- a mixture of embarrassment and chagrin.

I had been sent to Harbor Springs, Michigan, that summer, and the next thing I knew, it was the day before Christmas.

With me were Brother Anthony (Tony), a delightfully uncomplicated "shanty Irishman," and Father Rufinus (Roofie), a repatriated Chinese missionary who, even when he could still see out of both eyes, couldn't tell the difference between a Rembrandt and the happy face doodles of a third grader. My sense of the artistic left me in the position of being unable to criticize either of them.

In conjunction with the parish, there was a school. It was a day-school for local kids and a boarding school for Indian kids from all over the state of Michigan.

Seventeen Notre Dame Sisters cooked for, clothed, taught, and mothered the little Ottawas. For days before Christmas, they had been hauling trees into the big Indian school, setting them up in dormitories, dining rooms, corridors, classrooms, etc., etc., and, of course, decorating them in most tasteful ways.

Suddenly, the day before Christmas, it occurred to Brother A., Father R., and me that we didn't have a tree in our monastery. "Monastery" is a euphemism. We're talking about a monstrous, two-story, wooden shack that must have been built in the days of the Cro-Magnon man and then abandoned by him as being unfit for human habitation. The rats, bats, and mice, on the other hand, had not yet decided it was unfit for animal habitation.

So Brother A. dashed out to find a tree. What he came back with were pieces of trees, explaining that all the tree lots were sold out, and trees still standing were covered with snow. And besides, landowners took a dim view of people helping themselves to standing growths. We set about constructing our own tree out of the pieces.

An hour and a half later -- time that was filled with honest sweat, baling wire, binder twine, and ten-penny nails -- we were able to stand back and view our handiwork with pride.

In a burst of poetic emotion, I pointed out to Brother A. and Father R. that on one occasion, Kilmer had written the immortal lines: "... but only God can make a tree." But he had produced these words without having had the benefit of seeing what we had wrought. He would have considered his statement rash if he had been standing next to us at that moment.

Then the base of the tree slipped and the whole construction fell to the floor. We pushed it back up, leaned it into the corner of the living room and nailed the base to the floor. We straightened out the baubles and decoration (not all of them were broke in the accident), and left the angel at the top of the tree as it was, slightly off center and in a horizontal position.

We then went over to the convent and invited the Sisters to come and view the most unique Christmas tree they had ever seen. They filed into our living room and stood around the tree in awe-struck wonder. Finally, one ventured the remark: "It IS unique." Another said: "It is different." A third said she had never seen a Christmas tree like it in all her life.

Then, one in the crowd, who had a reputation for being outspoken, said: "Grotesque!" That encouraged others to speak their minds. Adjectives like "horrendous," "ghastly," "repulsive," and "ugly" were tossed around with reckless abandon until the quavering voice of old Sister Pientia on the edge of the crowd was heard to whisper: "Sacrilegious!" Then they all filed out with the veiled heads bowed, presumably to go to the convent chapel to say a prayer of reparation for the abomination they had just witnessed.

As if that weren't enough, my dachshund male puppy walked up to the tree, frowned, and made his comment -- as high as he could -- and then lay down in a corner, scowling like that tree was a personal insult to him.

You may think Brother A., Father R., and I were pretty chastened by now. Not so. We noted that there was a contest to determine who had the finest Christmas tree in town. We didn't enter the contest.

What we did was to announce at all the Masses at Christmas that the parish was invited to come into the monastery and see the ugliest Christmas tree in town. Large numbers responded. For the first time in its 150-year history, there was universal agreement on a subject. All accepted that judgment: "It is the ugliest Christmas tree in town." Some went further and included the whole county. Others extended it to the state and beyond.

By the next year, we were in a brand new monastery and one day, about the middle of Advent, the doorbell rang. Waiting outside were a group of Indian boys and a number of Sisters. They had a beautiful tree and decorations with them.

They marched in, set up the tree, and decorated it, keeping Tony and Roofie and me as far away from the action as possible. When they finished, the three of us stood before the tree and observed in one accord: "It just isn't the same as our old tree." There was universal agreement on that also.

Have at least a reasonably Merry Christmas, folks.

Eight Milking Maids

by Father Elstan
January 1987

Sorry you missed Al and Sue Orsen's annual party for the organ choir members. There was only one bleak spot in the whole evening.

When the goodies were safely stored away in the stomachs of those present and the egg nog was flowing freely, Sue sat down at the organ and Kathy Broberg divided us into a dozen equal groups. Then we launched into "The Twelve Days of Christmas."

With Sue's professional playing and under Kathy's excellent direction, we were progressing nicely -- until we came to Germaine Jesberg's line: a simple line really -- "Eight maids a-milking" – a line that the youngest in the family could commit to memory in a few minutes.

Germaine blew it. First she giggled. Then, in a tune no one could recognize, she sang, "Eight milking maids." Well, we didn't get back into our rhythm again until we went all the way around to Roger Leuthner who, in a rich bass voice, slowly sang his line: "Five golden rings."

After it was all over and the applause had subsided, someone (overlooking Germaine's contribution) suggested we go on the stage. Someone else, remembering Germaine's contribution, said, "Yeah, the first one going West."

This brings me to a subject that has exercised the old cerebellum every year at this time when "The Twelve Days of Christmas" starts to rise to the top of the charts again.

Who was this clown that had such a preoccupation with birds? What motivated him to send them to his girlfriend? What did he expect to accomplish? Couldn't he foresee the effect on this girl as she watched her tidy home being gradually transformed into a chicken coop?

These questions, and more, introduce mysteries as profound and deep as any contained in John's Book of the Apocalypse.

We can readily imagine the girl. (Let's call her Adeline in order to avoid getting all tangled up with pronouns in our composition. He will be Albert. We authors have to be clever in this regard.)

Anyway, Adeline responds to the partridge in a pear tree with all the enthusiasm and warmth of a young maiden's affection. Her responses express less and less gratitude as the days go on and the fowl accumulate.

Then came the five golden rings -- a welcome relief. Adeline pawns the rings to pay for the cleaning and repairs necessary in her once peaceful home.

Then Albert starts up with the birds again! And we can excuse Adeline if she refers to them in her letters to Albert as "turkeys," "ostriches," and "buzzards." She might even have called some of them "emus." Girls like Adeline in an overwrought condition might easily overlook the fine distinctions between species. She may even have begun to place Albert in an other-than-human species by this time. Girls are like that, you know.

So, to prove that he belonged where God created him, Albert introduced the human element, eight maids a-milking, or, according to Germaine's version, "eight milking maids." We presume they came with their cows.

These were followed, in order, by nine pipers playing, ten ladies dancing, and eleven lords a-leaping.

Let's assume the cows' digestive systems were in normal working order. That would explain the leaping lords and dancing ladies. They would have had to step lively to avoid the inevitable -- counting the birds in, too. As far as a bird is concerned, a floor is as good as a public statue.

By this time Adeline, whom we presume to have been a neat girl, and one who valued her privacy, must have been bringing the full force of her well-rounded vocabulary to bear in her responses to Albert's steady flow of ill-advised gifts. If one of those birds had been a sailor's parrot, we can see him hiding his beak under his wing and blushing profusely at Adeline's choice of words.

By the time the twelve fiddlers came fiddling, we can picture Adeline sitting in a well-padded cubicle staring wildly through the bars and removing large chunks of hair from her head. And Albert is in his lonely quarters, his head in his hands mumbling to himself, "Where did I go wrong?"

I shudder to think we must all go through attempting to fathom the mysteries contained in this episode again next year when the strains of "The Twelve Days of Christmas" hit the air waves and the sing-a-longs.

Until that time, enjoy '87 and, as the folks along the Mississippi Delta say, "See you next month -- God willin' an' the river don't rise."

The Abduction of Sissy

by Father Elstan
February 1987

There is little of universal interest that has transpired at St. Victoria's over the past month -- unless we consider two phone conversations I had that might give you food for thought.

You, as I, might wonder if A. G. Bell's purpose in begetting this instrument of communication is being fully realized. You might ask yourself, as I have, if it had not been well for him, and us, when he uttered those first historic words -- "Watson, come here. I want you ... " -- to have continued his message with the words: " ... to destroy this machine, tear up the patent, and never, ever divulge the secret of its operation to a soul!"

Consider the following incident.

Friends dropped in from out of state. I offered to take them out to dinner. They were delighted. I established a telephonic communication with a reasonably nice place within a half hour's driving distance.

"Hello. This is Sissy. Can I help you?"

"Yes. I would like to make reservations for four at 6 o'clock tonight, if I may."

"Reservations?! For dinner?" Her tone indicated this was a most unusual request.

"Yes. For dinner. What else do you make reservations for at this place?"

"Yeah. Right. Can you wait a sec?" And she passed out of my life. "Secs" developed into "mins," and "mins" were closing in on an "hr" when the voice of a callow youth, whose adenoids would have stimulated great interest in medical circles, drifted over the wire.

"Da! Is subwud od the lide?"

"Yes!!"

"Cad I help you?"

"Yes. But first you better call the police. I think Sissy has been abducted."

I shouldn't have said that. Adenoids Al indicated almost visible signs of life when I mentioned the word "police." I finally got him settled down and said, "I would like to make reservations for four at 6:30 if I may."

"Reservashuds? For four? To eat?"

"Yes. To eat. What else?"

"Yeah, ride. Cad you hold the lide for a biddut?"

"Why not?! I've held it so long now the receiver has grown to my ear!" While I was saying this, A. A. was drifting off to consult with higher authorities about this most extraordinary request he had just received over the "telephode."

So I waited and drummed out some rather catchy rhythms on the top of my desk with the fingers of my left hand as the sun slowly sank into the west and I watched my beard grow longer and cobwebs form on the receiver.

At long last, an efficient sounding voice came through. "Is there someone on this line?" -- to which I responded forthrightly: "Yes!"

"Can I help you?"

"I doubt it. No one else in this institution seems to be able to. I am attempting to make reservations for four at six thir...seven o'clock."

"Right! Now then ..." and I could hear him procuring the necessary forms, could almost see him licking the tip of his pencil, and we got down to business.

After obtaining my name, address, phone number, age, nationality and sex, and having been assured I had never engaged in subversive activities, nor been a member of the Communist party and was not suffering from any communicable disease, we concluded this most difficult part of the transaction.

I haven't mentioned the name of the eating place. I don't want to discourage anyone from going there. It is really a nice place. It was my misfortune to call at a time when the "B" team was in charge.

This thing has gotten longer than I expected and I wanted to tell you about another telephone experience I had about the same time. I'll save it for March. It will bolster any thesis that Mr. Bell's invention is not all it's cracked up to be.

In the meantime, if I can help you, call 443-2661.

Wristwatch Warfare

by Father Elstan
March 1987

I believe that last month's blurb gave you fair warning that I intended to record a second telephone conversation that occurred here at St. Victoria's recently. In an effort to strengthen any thesis that A. Bell's invention is frequently used for purposes other than simple communication, I submit the following:

The phone rang, as is its wont, and I answered in a way that is endorsed by both Miss Manners and Amy Vanderbilt. The right ear drum was immediately assailed by the following, spoken with all the enthusiasm of a TV evangelist soliciting funds.

"Ah, Father Elstan, I am so delighted I caught you at home and I must tell you how fortunate for you, Father Elstan, that I did. I am calling from Los Angeles, California, (and he said this like I should be impressed to get a phone call from *him* all the way from Los Angeles, California).

"I represent the well-known Remove-O Products Corporation, (products of such evident high quality certainly merit a well-thought-out name like that), and we have overstocked our inventory, so we are in a position to offer you, Father Elstan, any quantity of our Remove-O wax remover at a drastically reduced rate.

"As you undoubtedly know, Father Elstan, this high quality product comes in the handy five-gallon drum, and can take care of your wax build-up problems on hard surface floors quickly and cleanly.

"Our computer selected your name, Father Elstan, to be one of a very few to benefit from this generous offer. As a token of our appreciation in advance of your order we have already mailed, this very day, a beautiful wristwatch, your very own, free of charge, a gift to you from us."

This dude was just begging to have his leg pulled -- three yards from its moorings -- and I decided to accommodate him. So I answered, "This must be Divine Providence putting in overtime, George."

"That's Fred."

"Fred, yes, sorry. My computer must be functioning improperly. Just today I said to myself I must invest in a new wristwatch. My old Bulova is running out of time -- if you will excuse the bad joke, heh, heh. Does the wristwatch come with a guarantee?"

"Yes, yes ... Now, Father Elstan, how much hard surface flooring do you have at St. Victoria's?"

"About twelve square feet. Now, Ed ..."

"Fred."

"Oh, yes, Fred. Does this wristwatch come with a flexible band, snap-on band, or leather band or what?"

"Flexible ... With just twelve square feet of hard surface flooring you will probably want to order enough of our Remove-O to take care of your needs for years to come. As you know, when you order in quantity -- ten drums or more -- you receive five percent off of the original low price and we pay the shipping charges."

"Gee, that sounds too good to pass up ... To get back to the watch, is it rust-proof, shock-proof, and water-proof?"

"Yes, yes. All those things. Now, ... I have the order blanks before me here. How much shall I put you down for?"

Fred was manifesting a strange reluctance to dwell on the watch motif, but I surged ahead. "First tell me, will this wristwatch of which you speak so highly take a licking and keep on ticking?"

Fred hung up.

And the wristwatch hasn't arrived yet, due no doubt to the inefficiency of our postal system. Now, I ask you, is the telephone meant for that sort of thing?

I have more to say about the telephone. Do you believe that if A. Bell could have seen down the road to the time when tape recorders could be attached to his invention to give and receive messages, he would have unleashed it onto an unsuspecting public?

There is a growing volume of literature on just this subject to which I would like to add my bit. Irma Bombeck must have covered this topic, as has Andy Rooney, no doubt. I, as they, and millions of others, I'm sure, have suffered great indignities at the hands of these machines.

When a tape recorder answers my call, I wish it the time of day, inquire into its health, and that of the wife and kids, and then babble on inanely before emitting an hysterical giggle that suggests I am one brick short of a full load. And then, in all sincerity, I express the desire that it have a good day before hanging up.

Sometimes all this happens with appropriate music in the background -- "Silent Night" at Christmas time, "The Alleluia Chorus" during the Easter season, and "Lara's Theme" or a Strauss waltz in the time before Pentecost and the first Sunday in Advent.

I ask myself after hanging up from a scene as described above: Does God really expect us to suffer like that? What is the legislative branch of our government doing about this matter?

But, as I said last month, if I can be of any assistance to you, call 443-2661, and if a machine answers your call, and there is music in the background, call 911 and send the police.

Preparing for Pickles and Ice Cream

by Father Elstan
April 1987

When we find ourselves searching for a common ground for conversation, two subjects readily present themselves: a) the weather and, b) our pets. I am going to fall back on "b" for this month's dissertation.

As you may know, I have a nine pound, two-year-old toy dachshund who answers to the name "Maude" when she's hungry. Maude's zest for life led her to request an introduction to a male of her own size and species. I was put in touch with the Bob Johnsons in Jordan, the sister and brother-in-law of Sharon Lauwagie.

So, in the fullness of time, Maude and I hopped into the old Chev and headed for the queen city of Scott County. Arriving in due course at our chosen destination, we disembarked.

The Johnsons have a cat, a Pomeranian, horses, and two geese with the disposition of alligators being set upon by long, sharp instruments. And then, of course, there was Mac, also a toy dachshund, as dark and handsome a young chap as you will ever see that far away from a tropical beach.

Maude first asserted herself with the shy little Pomeranian lady, then checked to make sure the cat was sufficiently terrorized, and so turned her attention to the geese, continuing her impressive impersonation of a charter member of the Bader-Meinholf gang.

The geese retaliated with a credible recitation of steam escaping under high pressure. You've all seen a Disney cartoon where Goofy has to make a sudden stop to avoid disaster. His ears fly forward, his paws dig up about half a foot of turf, and his eyes register a combination of fear and surprise. Maude, on this occasion, could have been the model for his cartoon drawing. After skidding to a stop, she turned and fled to safety behind my size 10 Oxfords. She was peering from behind them when Mac came bounding over the rise to check out the commotion. All fears vanished.

There was no evidence of prejudice based on color (Mac is about three shades darker than Maude), so a marriage was arranged and I departed to leave Mac and Maude with the sunset on the ruins of the old brewery and to discover together the surpassing beauty of algae growing over the old mill pond.

Two weeks later I went back to the Johnsons' to bring Maude home and, if what I learned in Biology II, and the fact that she has been demanding pickles and ice cream for breakfast have any validity, I should be able to report exciting news by the end of April or the first part of May. Till then ...

Gestating Mightily

by Father Elstan
May 1987

There are bits and pieces of news from St. Victoria this month.

Just before Easter there was a crew from the Hartman Tree Farm swarming all over the yard here, busier than a bunch of brick layers in Beirut. They completed the landscaping work that was begun last summer by the cement work in the front of the church and on the new sidewalks.

The entire project was financed by Mr. and Mrs. Robert Dahlin -- the cement work, the new trees and bushes, the new grass, the landscaping; and we thank them. We also thank Kenny Diethelm and Tony Kerber who have been keeping the new plantings well watered (no pun intended there).

Our gratitude goes to the Michel men, Gerald and James, as well. Last Saturday they took a chain saw in one hand and their life in the other and scrambled up into the bowels of the big maple tree outside my office window, acting remarkably like a couple of primates as they cleared out the dead branches.

I would like to be able to report something of a positive nature with regard to Maude and her puppy (puppies). As of this writing, she continues to gestate mightily, but the results of her efforts will have to be reported at a future date. Be patient and try not to worry unduly.

If I had anything to do with it, I would be bragging shamelessly about the music at St. V's over Holy Week and at the Easter Masses provided by Sue and her Crew, and Jerry and Kathy and the dedicated artists in their group.

And, on Wednesday of Holy Week, a gaggle of gals with spring house-cleaning in mind descended on the church like a bunch of agitated wasps!! No speck of dust could possibly survive the onslaught -- nor did it.

Stay tuned for a final report on results of Maude's efforts.

Mechanical Mysteries

by Father Elstan
June 1987

One time, years ago, in an age that would be termed "antiquity," a saintly, scholarly man, having observed the human scene for a long time, sagaciously observed: "Everyone has his/her cross to bear." The old boy hit the nail on the head.

My own personal cross is having been granted an IQ in matters mechanical that just slightly exceeds that of an earthworm's. When something of a mechanical nature involves any principle more sophisticated than a paper clip, I've had it.

If there is some machine I have to deal with that has moving parts and I get too close to that machine, one or more of the parts fall off. If operation of the machine calls for punching a button, and there are two or more buttons, I unerringly punch the wrong one, usually with devastating results.

When my automobile ceases to function and I contact a garage, their first question is always: "What's wrong with it?" The best I can do is to respond knowingly: "It doesn't work." Oh, I've come up with some facetious answers like: "The generator doesn't generate, the carburetor doesn't carburate, and the pistons don't work" or "The magneto seems to have become disengaged from the knuten rod."

But to give an answer that is of any practical help is beyond my ability. Then I stand by and watch with wide-eyed wonder as he or she flicks open the hood (an operation that would have taken me ten minutes and resulted in three scraped knuckles), peers into the entrails of the machine, blows a little dust off the radiator cap, twiddles a wire and turns a screw one and one-third times, and the car takes off like a bloodhound that has just had a generous helping of turpentine judiciously applied to his person. How do they do it???

This cross of mine has resulted in a number of embarrassments over the years. In the '60's I bought one of the earlier models of Volkswagens. It was my kind of machine, simple of design, reliable, trouble-free. I drove it for two years without ever doing anything more complicated to it than filling it with fuel.

Then one day I pulled up to the drive-in window of the bank. There were several cars ahead of me, so I turned off the motor to wait my turn. When it came, I engaged the key -- and nothing happened. The cars behind me were expressing some impatience with their horns, all of which seemed to be in good working order.

One can't just sit there under these circumstances, so I did what everybody else does when their car stalls -- I looked under the hood. It became immediately evident to me why the motor wouldn't start. There was no motor.

Applying the full force of that part of the mind that governs our perception of mechanical principles, I concluded: "There has to be one somewhere. How did I drive this thing for the past two years?"

So I instituted a thorough search and, finally, found the motor in the trunk. By this time a large crowd had gathered, watching my movements with great interest and mounting curiosity. My advice to the public is -- if you are driving a Volkswagen, to avoid unbearable chagrin, always keep foremost in your mind, the spare tire is where the motor should be and vice-versa.

Now, to touch on another matter, it seems my perception of biological principles is no better than my grasp of mechanical mysteries ...

For those of you who are waiting with mounting concern, Maude is "unpregnant." It's a simple case of having counted our chickens before they were hatched. I can't explain it. It's just the way it is. And so, back to the drawing board at some future date. Be patient. One more cross we must bear bravely.

The Old Son of the Soil
And the Young Whippersnapper

by Father Elstan
July 1987

The time has come to speak out fearlessly about an ever-growing, modern trend that is affecting us all. I refer to the tendency we all seem to experience since the Second Vatican Council to classify everybody as a far left radical or a far right conservative.

I, myself, have been referred to, in the same day, by those of widely differing views as a blood-spitting, bearded Bolshevik and as one mired up to my armpits in the muck of Victorian reactionism.

The fact is, I believe, both extremes are wrong, and sometimes dangerous. In support of that thesis, I submit the following example:

Years ago, when I was growing up on the farm, we had two neighbors whose lands were adjacent. The one was an old son of the soil who was also an old stick-in-the-mud (conservative). The other was a young whippersnapper (radical).

The one was the "first by whom the new was tried" -- the other, "the last to lay the old aside." And they were in a constant altercation about who should erect the line fence between the two properties.

There appeared at this time in all the farmers' publications, to none of which did our older conservative friend subscribe, extensive information on, and praise of, the merits of a new kind of fence, consisting of one simple wire, charged with electricity and most effective in keeping the cows, horses, and pigs confined within the area defined by it.

Our young, progressive farmer recognized the superiority of this type of fence over the old conventional three or four strands of barbed wire anchored to heavy posts. He bought a large supply, and when he had his whole farm fenced in by the new method, had enough left over to run a line fence between his property and his neighbor's.

About the time the work was completed, the old man came out to see what was going on, and, when he saw, made inquiries. Told that it was a line fence, and they could now lay their hassle to rest, he expressed his views on one-strand fences that weren't even barbed, using his vast and colorful vocabulary.

Not satisfied that he had made his point clear by mere words, he mentioned his intention to take action, to leave no doubt about where he stood in the matter. Since the wire was handy, and he had to go to the men's room anyway, and this would be a graphic demonstration of his contempt, he prepared to use the wire as a facility.

The young man recognized the hazards involved in this procedure and hastened, in a spirit of true altruism, to say, "You'd better not!" The old man misinterpreted the remark to be a threat, and nobody, by golly, was going to threaten him. He advanced to carry out his nefarious scheme.

Reports vary with regard to exactly what they heard spoken at the time of this historic event. Some say they heard him remark: "QX!@*Z&#!!" Others merely recall hearing, "QX."

That there should be any discrepancy at all in these reports is extraordinary, because all witnesses agree his clear tenor voice, ringing out over the hills and valleys, was audible over an area of seventeen townships. (Some say sixteen.)

We chroniclers of these momentous events strive for accuracy, but in this case it seems we will have to wait for the day of judgment to find out exactly what the old man said, and precisely how far his voice carried.

But the essential element of the event is there for all to learn from -- namely, extremes of conservatism are not only erroneous, but can be perilous. Perhaps next month we can explore the dangers of extreme progressivism.

The Dedicated Loafer

by Father Elstan
August 1987

If you throw your mind back to last month's St. Victoria's news, you will recall our having put forth a thesis that extreme ideological positions are usually erroneous and frequently harmful.

In defense of that claim we explored the results of a far right (conservative) approach to life and its painful consequences. In fairness, and for the sake of a proper balance, we shall delve into the perils of extreme left wing (radical) leanings by means of an example.

In our neighborhood, which was replete with "originals," Old Lars Larson stood head and shoulders above them all in those qualities which set him aside as a unique "character." (The name has been changed to protect me.)

I don't know what it was about our locality that spawned these extraordinary men. Some claimed it had to do with the soil. Others theorized that swamp gases drifting up out of the peat bogs and lowlands along the Minnesota River had a beneficial influence. Whatever the causes, Lars had been deeply affected by them.

Lars was not by nature a soap box radical, nor a confirmed conservative. What he was by nature was a dedicated loafer, and any idea that came along with a promise of easing his work load, he subscribed to with boundless enthusiasm.

The county agent pointed out to him that he would find it much easier to milk his herd of Holsteins if he were to apply fly spray before milking. He did so with high expectations.

The spray worked. It was easier and more pleasant milking his eighteen head, but after several days he grew weary of spraying all those cows and had begun to wonder if it wouldn't be easier to skip the spraying and bear the burden of switching and kicking cows.

He was comparing the relative merits of his two possible choices when the lights went on. "If a little spray lasts a few hours, a lot will last longer. A whole lot will last indefinitely." (Lars applied the same reasoning process to home brew and corn likker: If a little made him feel good, a lot would make him feel better.)

So he bought a few five-gallon barrels of the concoction, soaked some rags in it, brought along a dipper and proceeded to bathe the cattle in those places where the flies and mosquitoes congregated in large and hungry numbers for their evening repast.

It would be unfair to say that Lars' experiment was a total loss. His intention was to ease his burden of heavy work. The means he chose did that. After losing all their hair, the cows stopped giving milk, and several of them gave up the ghost. Lars didn't have to do any spraying or milking for the rest of the summer.

But I believe the point is made: Extremely radical approaches can result in disaster to all concerned, and we do not recommend it as a philosophy by which to guide your life's course.

Mary and the Sandburrs

by Father Elstan
September 1987

A couple of months ago there was a party at the St. Victoria Parish Center, given for 65 or 70 people who contribute extra time and effort to the parish programs. Toward the end of the evening, one of the celebrants with a gift for words summed up the evening by coining the phrase: "A good time was had by all."

As I stepped out the door to the parking lot after the revels, I observed a number of the younger element gathered in conspiratorial conference. After some discreet interrogations it was revealed that one of the members of our party was celebrating her birthday, and her "friends" had collected all the plastic forks, knives, and spoons from the meal with the object of slipping, under cover of darkness, into her yard and planting the above mentioned items in an upright position in a random pattern all over her lawn.

I walked back to my house recalling some of the practical jokes of which I had been in the past a victim, a participant, or an observer, and recalled what some great mind had once sagaciously observed (although his observation didn't apply in this case) that most practical jokes are neither practical nor jokes.

And I harked back to the time I was in the fourth grade when an apparently harmless stunt could have wiped out a large segment of the school age population of our neighborhood; and I'm sure the perpetrator of the act did not foresee the possible consequences of it.

On our meandering home from school each day, after hours spent in the pursuit of higher learning, our journey took us past a sand pit where three men toiled with mallets and shovels and dynamite to break up the sandstone and load it onto box cars.

One of these men, known to us as "Old Fierce Fritz," adopted a singular attitude toward children. He saw little need for them. He had heard W. C. Field's observation that "anyone who hates little children can't be all bad," and subscribed to that philosophy wholeheartedly.

He looked into the future and saw scant hope for it when he observed those who represented it. And he made it abundantly clear to us by word and gesture where he stood on the subject of children -- merely because he lost his shovel one time and suspected us of hiding it behind the bush where he found it, and merely because he happened to be in the little tin shack one time where the men kept their tools and where they ducked into when they set off a charge of dynamite at the same time we chose to throw racks up against the metal walls to obtain a unique sound effect -- and other incidents real and imagined -- hardly justified his extraordinary view of the young. But that's the way it was.

On this warm day in May we, about a dozen of us, came by the sand pit. The men were down there with their heads about two feet below us as we stood on the edge and plied them with questions in our continuing search for knowledge.

"Old Fierce Fritz" was just below us and, with his back to us, bent over his shovel. As he grumbled and growled and we quizzed and chattered, my younger sister, Mary, with the cool deliberation of one of the "Dirty Dozen," picked up a handful of sand and sandburrs and, aiming amazingly accurately, poured the content down between his sweat-beaded neck and his protruding shirt collar.

The significance of this ill-advised action escaped none of us. We got off the mark quickly and concentrated on setting the record for the hundred yard dash for those between the ages of six and twelve -- all except Mary. She calmly turned around and skipped along, swinging her books and lunch pail, wearing an angelic expression and humming a hymn she recalled from her First Communion Day. It worked.

Mary's portrayal of angelic innocence camouflaged the murky blackness of her soul. O. F. Fritz, with imprecations on his lips and mayhem in his heart (and sand down his back), charged past her in hot pursuit of us who were more apparently guilty.

To put your mind at rest, he didn't catch any of us. A cheetah in mid-season form could not have caught us. He finally turned around and returned to the scene of his labors, walking right past Mary, who was still skipping and singing and swinging her books and lunch pail, he expressing some rather original views on the subject of modern youth.

I shall submit other examples in the future to bolster the contention: Most practical jokes are neither practical nor jokes.

Two Carp for Leonard

by Father Elstan
October 1987

There is more to be said on the subject introduced in this column last month. If you throw your mind back to that scholarly presentation, you will remember we introduced the premise that most practical jokes are neither jokes nor practical.

The following, though droll to some, had little practical value, and could have resulted in a degree of physical harm to your correspondent.

Some months ago you read in this column about a neighbor of ours, Lars Larsen, who lost his dairy herd because he gave them an overdose of fly spray. Lars had a son, Leonard, and between the two of them they provided most of the material for conversations in the local bars and barber shops.

Leonard drove a car -- though it was never referred to as a "car" by those who discussed the subject. It could not be identified as to make and model because it was pieced together from parts of many makes and models. What held the pieces together remains to this day a deep mystery.

It was draped with a profusion of license plates of various dates -- none of which were current. As Leonard lurched along the corrugated gravel roads of Scott and adjacent counties, everything on the vehicle made noise except the horn, which, of course, didn't work.

One hot August afternoon my brother and I, and a couple of local lads, dug up some worms -- grub and angle -- and headed, with the necessary equipment, to our fishing spot on Sand Creek. We were attempting to coax the elusive bullhead to bite.

We hauled in two fair-sized carp and threw them into the high grass on the creek bank. In due time, Leonard rattled up behind us in his hybrid machine. He immediately began to dispense his invaluable advice to us on how to attach the bait, how deep to fish, where to drop the line in the water, etc., etc.

A brilliant and, I thought, original idea hit me like a divine inspiration. While Leonard was preoccupied with his kindly mission of imparting his invaluable knowledge to the others, I slipped around to the trunk of his vehicle, opened it by untying the binder twine that held it shut, and deposited one of the carp inside one of the tires stored there -- a tire whose condition suggested it would never be used again on a wheel.

The day wore on. Eventually Leonard took his noisy leave and the rest of us started home. After a few yards down the road my brother sidled up to me, dug his elbow into my ribs in a conspiratorial manner, and said, "Guess what I did."

The moment he said it, I instinctively knew. "Oh, no! Where did you hide yours?" -- "Under the gunny sacks on the back seat."

The long summer were on. At the end of August I left for the seminary outside of Chicago. Shortly afterwards Leonard skidded into our yard in a cloud of dust, looking for the two of us. He had thought and reasoned, and come to some conclusions, based mostly on the shaky reputation my brother and I already had in the neighborhood.

My brother's instincts for self preservation stood him in good stead. He told Leonard that I had perpetrated the crime, that I was in Chicago studying to be a priest, that I wouldn't be home for months, and that he, my brother, had been appalled when I told him what I had done. The deed has gone unpunished to this day.

The contemplation of the possible consequences of that ill-advised action have helped me down through the years to be cautious of inspirations that seemed at first blush to be of divine origin.

The Most Delicious Crow

by Father Elstan
November 1987

My original intention for this month's column had been to give you the benefit of some more practical jokes with which I have been associated, but since the last issue of the *Gazette* hit the newsstands, events of such momentous consequence have transpired I feel constrained to comment on them.

I refer, of course, to the recent happenings in the Metrodome.

I confess to having developed over the years a pessimistic approach to all forms of sport in Minnesota. After suffering through four futile superbowls, the feeble efforts of the Golden Gophers, the bridesmaid status of the North Stars, and the hilarious antics of the Twins for so long, the possibility of ever being in the position of backing a winner seemed out of the question.

So I enjoyed the games by watching for what could be ridiculed, and laughing in order to keep from crying, watching Kent Hrbek try to stretch a hit into a double (for anybody else it would have been a triple) by sliding into second on his stomach and not getting stopped till he was out in center field -- and getting thrown out, of course; watching Kirby Puckett wander off first base and while he was standing there picking his nose and staring into space (probably dreaming about being in the World Series), getting thrown out by the catcher; watching them go into the ninth inning seven runs ahead and losing the game, etc., etc.

One long laugh after the other, until they stumbled into the Western Division Championship, sailed through the American League pennant, and I was beginning to think of all the crow I might have to eat, just maybe. And I was willing to eat it if need be.

And I devised a means of helping them win. It is a fact of life that when I bet on something, it is bound to blow a fuse, so I decided to bet against the Twins in every game.

I wagered 25 cents on every game with Fathers Cochran, Val, and our cook, Mrs. Fiebelkorn, and it paid off -- in a manner of speaking. The whole business cost me about three and a half bucks, but what a small price to pay for being a part of a World Champion team.

And now the business of the crow. Excuse me while I say grace in preparation for partaking of the most delicious crow ever consumed by man or vulture.

The Dummy on the Tower

by Father Elstan
December 1987

Now that the bragging over the World Series has subsided and our pride in Minnesota has been restored by the results of that series, it is time to return to subjects of a more profound nature.

You may recall that this column was presenting a number of examples of events that bolster my contention that many practical jokes are neither jokes nor practical. The following might well not have been either if the victims of it had been inclined to faint easily.

It happened when I was stationed in Columbus, Nebraska. On the outskirts of a neighboring town, a large radio tower was under construction. It was so tall it was being celebrated in song and story, and measured against the World Trade Center, Mount Everest, and professional basketball players.

As the work progressed, the men on the job noticed that every day about noon an elderly couple from town drove out, parked near the construction and watched them as they climbed up and down the ever-growing structure, and ate their braunschweiger sandwiches and emptied their thermos bottle as they watched -- an understandable mid-day diversion for a couple of retired people.

An inspiration, the kind that comes only rarely, struck one of the workmen. He fixed up a dummy and hauled it to the top of the tower. Then he placed workers at various levels the full length of the structure; and in the tall grass at the base of the tower, he had one of the men conceal himself with proper instructions.

Noon came. The old folks arrived, and were watching contentedly when the figure of a man plunged from the precarious height. As it fell past the men along the length of the structure, each one at the proper time screamed appropriately.

The figure landed with a sickening thud, sending the Nebraska sand into the air well above the tall grass.

The workman, lying in the grass next to where the overalls stuffed with straw and fixed with a head and shoes landed, jumped up, dusted himself off and yelled to the men at the top of the tower, "If you guys don't quit fooling around up there, I'm going to quit this job!" And he started to climb to the top.

The fate of the two interested on-lookers has never been disclosed.

St. Victoria Church News

from Editor Sue
January 1988

Father Elstan's column will return next month when he's feeling better.

Where Will It All End?

by Father Elstan
February 1988

Let's expend one more column on the subject of practical jokes. All too often they stimulate retaliation and we eventually are faced with the obvious question: "Where will it all end?"

I was stationed in Harbor Springs, Michigan, and one winter night, when the snow was high and the thermometer was low, two couples in a covered Jeep picked me up to take me to a Chamber of Commerce meeting. After the meeting we stopped at a popular watering hole for a cup of hot chocolate, and to say all the things we should have said at the meeting.

Presently, another young couple on their way out stopped at our table to say "Hi," etc., etc., and left. They also left our driver with an uneasy feeling. This couple had a reputation of using their imaginations to interrupt the smooth tenor of people's lives.

Suddenly our driver jumped up mumbling, "I wonder. I just wonder!" -- and rushed outside. Too late! The Jeep was clear full of "Michigan dandruff." He came back and invited us to help him clear the vehicle out, which we did; and as we did, we discussed a proper form of vengeance.

Someone suggested that on a cold night like this, if you pour hot water around the tires of a parked vehicle, said vehicle would stay put till the spring thaw. We endorsed this happy solution, acquired two large dish pans full of hot water from our host, and set out in search of the enemy. They had vanished into thin air. They weren't even at their house when they should have been.

Wet, weary, and seething with indignation, we came back to the parish house and pondered our problem.

Suddenly it hit me! I had just recently read about someone who wanted to demonstrate the difference between "irritation," "anger," and "violent rage." He selected a phone number at random at 11 p.m., called and said, "Is Joe there?"

Being informed he had a wrong number, he waited two hours and called the same number and presented the same question. He was emphatically informed he had a wrong number. Two hours later he called again and said, "This is Joe. Have there been any phone calls for me?"

We forged ahead, assigning a time to each of the groups to call at two-hour intervals starting that night, going through the next day and through the following night. We all inquired about a mythical "Bill Simpson." The last call was from Mr. Simpson himself.

It worked as planned, but our group has been uneasy ever since. "When will the ax fall?" we keep asking. We rest uneasily. Sudden noises startle us unduly. I'm beginning to wonder whom the joke is on. Is their plan to do nothing in return and let us stew? Where will it all end?

No Snakes in the Emerald Isle

by Father Elstan
March 1988

Sue called to remind me of the *Gazette* deadline. Panic gripped my heart. I hadn't an idea. She suggested, since it was the month of the Feast of St. Patrick, I might want to discuss nationalities --Irish, in particular, or my own national origins, or the saint himself. I don't think so, except for a few remarks that you might find helpful.

Whatever St. Patrick was, he was not Irish. Various nationalities claim him, including my own which is Scotch. He came to the Irish as a missionary from some place, but not from Ireland.

Some years ago, the church attempted to correct unlikely stories that have grown up around this saint, and has subsequently been accused of kicking him off the exclusive roster of the canonized. (She got in hot water over the same problem with St. Christopher.)

Among other accomplishments for which St. Patrick is given credit is that he drove the snakes from the Emerald Isle. Not so. There have never been nor are there presently any snakes of any kind in that land -- except in the visions and imaginations of some of her more dedicated imbibers.

Stories abound about the length of his prayers -- and the number of them that he said in the course of a day. Some scholar added up the time necessary to say those prayers and found that the total time far exceeded the 24 hours that is the length of a day in Ireland, as it is every place else.

Many of the accounts had him standing in ice cold water up to his neck while he said all those prayers. Unless he was the subject of a continually ongoing miracle, he could not have survived one day, much less a lifetime, under those conditions.

And if all those tales were true, when would he have had time to implant the faith so deeply in the hearts of the pagan Celts, the druid priests, and the O'Briens? Well, I mean, let's be realistic. One of the many delightful traits of the Irish is to take a good story and make it better and, in the case of St. Patrick, they really outdid themselves.

Well, now, here I've rambled on so long with "a few remarks" about St. Patrick that it's inadvisable to go on with the real subject I intended to discuss, which was "some Irishmen I have known." Actually, that could take some time and space, so I'll reserve that bit till next month. Have a Happy St. Patrick's Day!

A Prize from Blue Ribbon Bulls

by Father Elstan
April 1988

Maybe it's in our genes. Maybe it's coincidence. Maybe a sociologist could explain it, but I find the parallel between what happened to my brother Jesse and me extraordinary.

You may recall I commandeered this column some months ago to relate to you a phone conversation with a company in Los Angeles who called to tell me of my remarkable good fortune in their having come up with my name on their computer which made me a candidate for an astoundingly generous offer.

They had, a friendly salesman said, already put in the mail a valuable watch as a gift in appreciation of my anticipated order (large) of their wax remover product, something no institution should be without. In the course of my trying to ascertain the various features of the watch, our conversation was interrupted and the opportunity to save high sums of money eluded me.

I was telling my brother about my misfortune and he said he had had a similar experience. This offer came through the mail and entailed a prize and product that would save him vast amounts of money and make him the envy of all his neighbors.

He felt constrained to respond to the offer by mail. I asked him if he could recall what he wrote. He could, and gave me a copy of his response. It reads as follows ...

"Sirs: Words cannot express the thrill and joy I experienced upon hearing that my name came up on your computer, thus making me eligible for your product and prize. However, I will not be able to claim that prize nor place an order for your product as I am presently going through bankruptcy. You see, I invested all my worldly wealth in scrap metal and the market collapsed. Oh, well, easy come, easy go.

"But don't despair, my friends, as you are in luck. You see, your name came up on MY computer, and, guess what! Yes, you are a winner of a prize with no strings attached. And what is this prize, you ask, as you well might.

"Let me tell you, old buddy, it is something you and your staff can relate to, as I'm sure you have had a lot of experience with it. It's something you can use every day, it makes a great conversation piece, and it's a thing of beauty and a joy forever.

"And the prize -- are you ready for this? Yes, it's 1,000 pounds -- I say one-half ton -- of well aged barnyard manure, the byproduct of my best blue ribbon bulls. It will be arriving at your office very soon by special delivery. You will probably know the prize is coming when it gets within a mile of your office if the wind is right.

"At any rate, keep your eyes and nose open and enjoy. Who knows, maybe next month you may be the big winner of our grand sweepstakes -- ten tons of the same."

Now, isn't that worth noting -- blood brothers both offered a once-in-a-lifetime opportunity, and both being unable to benefit from that opportunity because of circumstances.

Say la vie!

A Lucky Strike at the Prison

by Father Elstan
May 1988

Shortly after the publication of last month's *Gazette*, I received an envelope with a Minneapolis postmark. In the envelope was the article from this space with black angry lines drawn through it and the remark: "At least for EASTER you could be spiritual" written across the top of the page and the question: "Where is the Resurrection?" written across the bottom of the page.

My correspondent neglected to sign his name so I have to answer his question here by referring him to the four Gospels and the Acts of the Apostles for a masterful account of the Resurrection.

As for being "spiritual" -- Well! I'd like you to know I'm just as spiritual as the next guy. In fact, I had a spiritual experience once -- in 1957 -- that I'm sure will bolster my contention.

I was stationed at Guardian Angels in Chaska at the time. One day I received a bulky envelope from Father Conran Schneider who was located in Ashland, Wisconsin, at the time.

In the envelope was a lengthy questionnaire pertaining to a marriage case he was working on. He asked me to present the questions to a young woman who, at the time, was a guest at the ladies' reformatory in Shakopee.

As a professional courtesy I called the chaplain of the institution to inform him I would be interviewing a member of his flock. He said: "I'm glad you called first. When you walk into the place, you will be confronted by a woman who is excessively inquisitive. She will bombard you with questions. Don't tell her anything more than your name, rank and serial number."

I thanked him for the warning, hung up, and headed for Shakopee. I walked in the door of the place to which the chaplain had directed me. Behind the desk sat a huge female. She was wearing a large uniform of some kind and filling it out completely. Her head looked like ten acres of ripe oats. Her features suggested the blood of a thousand Viking ancestors was flowing in her veins.

And the thought crossed my mind as I took it all in: "This one could play in the line of one of Knute Rockne's better football teams."

My thought was interrupted by her rather curt question: "Who are you?" I said, "Father Elstan! Who are you?" And she announced abruptly: "Evelyn Rockne!"

It took me a moment to absorb this. Then I said: "Any relation to Knute?" And again, equally abruptly: "First cousin!"

Well -- I mean -- if that doesn't rate a seven point three on the Richter scale of spiritual experiences, I don't know what does.

With that, she proceeded with the third degree -- a process she was well versed in, and as I had been warned she would.

One doesn't tell one who wears an imposing uniform, and who is related to Knute Rockne, and looks like a contender for the ladies' heavyweight wrestling championship that this or that is none of her business, but as discreetly as possible I got it across that the only information I could divulge was that I had to present this questionnaire to a resident under her care.

Finally she said: "Okay … Come with me and I'll get her for you."

I toddled along behind her as she marched me to a parlor-like room. She pointed a muscular finger at the room and said: "Go in there and when I bring her in, leave the door open!"

I must have looked like I was going to make a remark about that directive because she said immediately: "For YOUR protection, not hers."

Then she marched off in a military fashion and I waited with fear and trepidation. Presently Ms. Rockne returned with a strikingly pretty young lady in tow. She showed her into the room and departed.

Though pretty, my companion wore the expression of one who was accustomed to telling Al Capone where to head in; and when I got down to the questions in the document, I expected her to spit out of the corner of her mouth before answering.

Well, she didn't. In fact, she wouldn't answer any of the questions at all. She said: "What's it to ya?" a lot, and "Nuts!" and "The heck with it!" and terse phrases like that. We were getting no place.

Suddenly I noticed a large sign on the wall: "No Smoking!" I asked her if they were serious about that command. She said, "Yeah! We can't do nothin' in here."

I suggested we ignore the sign. I produced a pack of Lucky Strikes, offered her one and lit one for myself. A light went on behind her tough mask and she answered the questions from then on, employing colorful and descriptive words -- some of which I was hearing for the first time in my life.

After the interview, I got what could best be described as an inspiration. I offered my friend the rest of the pack. She snatched them so fast and made them disappear so fast, I was astounded. And I left with a delicious sense of wicked conspiracy having just violated one of the institution's most sacred restrictions virtually under the very nose of the ever-vigilant and imposing Evelyn Rockne.

Fr. Pancratius Panfisch Visits Jordan

by Father Elstan
June 1988

I feel somewhat remiss in not divulging "St. Victoria Church News" in this column, but our faithful editor faithfully reports such faithful events as our Catholic Aid meetings and other items of gripping interest in the *Gazette* and to its vast reading public. And I have reported them in our weekly bulletin.

Besides, my brother would never forgive me if I were to report these stirring events in detail, because when we were kids we took great delight in opening up the local paper every week, *The Jordan Independent*, and reading the social page that reported faithfully the fact that the "third cousin of Mrs. Myrtle Migrain visited her at 3:30 p.m. on the 10th and was served tea and cake while a pleasant conversation was held. At 4:47 p.m. the above-mentioned relative, Mrs. Hortense Hauenbrager, took her leave and returned to her home in Saskatoon, Saskatchewan, Canada."

He, my brother, always felt constrained to speculate what the conversation was about, why Mrs. Hauenbrager took an abrupt leave at 4:47 p.m., and how long it would be before we were treated to an account of another visit to the pleasant home of Mrs. Migrain by another fascinating personality.

But the time came when he was faced with the possibility of just retribution for his wicked glee. It was when my father died and, after the funeral, it fell to his lot to hand in a report of the funeral to the editor of the *Independent.*

This editor was intent on details, prided himself on his journalistic integrity, and copied down carefully what was reported to him.

There were about fourteen Franciscan friars present for the funeral, scarcely any of whom did my brother know. But he did know that many of our Franciscan brothers were burdened with some outlandish names.

After mentioning my name and a few others that had to be authentic, he concocted the rest. "Present for the funeral were Father Pancratius Panfisch, O.F.M.; Father Ildephons Illenbed, O.F.M.; Brother Eusebius Usabus, O.F.M.;

etc., etc." and finally, "Father Joe Smith, O.F.M., from New York City, New York."

The editor reported these names as given. My mother spent the next six months explaining who these people were, and my brother went on to develop a hobby of inventing occasions and events which he periodically handed in for publication.

Historians at some future date will run across these names and events and attempt to verify them, and wind up in heavily upholstered rooms strumming their lips with their index fingers and humming soft music to themselves.

If, however, Maude or Frieda do something spectacular over and above their routine rowdy behavior, or if one of the members of the church has their cause for canonization presented in Rome, or another skunk comes along and prompts Julianne to call out the National Guard, you will be the first to hear about it -- in this column.

St. Victoria Church News

from Editor Sue
July 1988

Fr. Elstan is vacationing in the Great Northwest

Snoring through the Black Hills

by Father Elstan
August 1988

I just know that you of the *Gazette's* vast reading public are waiting for a detailed description of my recent vacation to the Great Northwest, but I have opted against trying to satisfy your curiosity. My decision, arrived at after much serious thought and soul-searching, is based on an experience I suffered through some fifteen years ago.

A parishioner and his wife invited Father Rufinus and me to an evening meal in their home. It was an excellent German-style meal, and, upon conclusion, we settled into easy chairs in the living room for some pleasant conversation before going home.

But, just about the time our hostess was finishing the dishes and we were finishing a shot of schnapps, the master of the house announced he had a great evening of entertainment planned for us.

He explained that recently he had loaded the wife and kids into the car and set out on the adventure of a lifetime -- a trip to the Black Hills. Since this was such a momentous event, it had to be captured on film for the benefit of his friends and relatives and so the "kids will have something to show their kids," so he had taken his 16 mm camera along.

As he went about setting up the screen and stringing the film, I noticed his children all excused themselves and went their various ways, and his wife chose an easy chair behind the projector in a dark corner and assumed a resigned expression.

I thought I detected substantially less enthusiasm on their part than on his -- and so sought out a remote corner in the dark. Father Roofie (which was what we in the order all called Fr. Rufinus) was not so lucky. He got a chair within easy view of the Entertainment Committee.

The camera rolled and the show began, with a complete commentary for each scene. There was a picture of the back end of the car with one of the kids running around it, and since it was impossible to tell which one, we were let in on the mystery and also given the child's quote as he ran.

There was a picture taken from the moving car which called for details missing in the picture, but provided by the technician at the controls, revealing that that particular shot was taken 33 1/2 miles west of Sioux Falls ... or was it 40 miles ... maybe closer to 35. "Ma, how far out of Sioux Falls was that?"

Another classic was of a jackrabbit bounding over the horizon. I know it was a jackrabbit because he pointed it out on the screen with a yardstick and told us he had seen it clearly before he managed to get it in the lens.

Another feature of this short was a tumbleweed that drifted into camera range at the time and he was just lucky to be running the camera when it happened.

Comic relief was provided by a short of a farmer trudging across the yard to his outdoor biffy. "I was just lucky to be coming along at the time and getting the shot." The living room rocked with laughter -- mostly our host's.

And so the thrilling adventure progressed until there was the sound of a pit full of agitated rattlesnakes. The film broke, or slipped off the cogs, or something. The commentary went on during the repair work.

I'm sorry to have to relate I missed most of the "real stuff," the documentary on the Black Hills themselves. I say "most of it" because I was aroused from a pleasant slumber occasionally by the snores emanating from Roofie's vast interior.

And there was one thrilling scene everybody witnessed -- it was when the film caught fire.

At length, the extravaganza came to a climax and conclusion. We, Roofie and I, aroused ourselves to depart, with expressions of sincere gratitude for the meal and somewhat less sincere expressions of thanks for the show.

Several months after this night of delight, I met the family outside the church. She asked me cautiously if I would like to come up to the house for a meal again some time. I said I would be delighted, and then asked casually, "Have you been on any trips lately?"

So, rather than tell you about my trip, I would like to leave you with some advice. If you are really interested in the majestic beauty of the Canadian Rockies and peaceful splendor of Lake Louise, take out a subscription to the *National Geographic.*

Corporal Punishment
In the Cloakroom

by Father Elstan
September 1988

The inexcusable march of time finds us on the brink of another school year.

Parents and principals, teachers and administrators are consulting with each other and with "experts" to search out the best means to impart the most knowledge to the resisting subjects.

One area of concern is always discipline: who should apply it, how much should be applied, and when and where in order to bring about the best results with the least amount of damage to the psyches of the recipients.

In a simpler age simple solutions were used. All concerned knew who did the applying to whom and what deserved it.

In my school, St. John's in Jordan, every classroom was supplied with a cloakroom. Everybody wore cloaks in those days. The girls wore girls' cloaks; the boys were boys' cloaks. The girls' cloaks were hung on one side of the cloakroom, the boys' on the other.

But there was a secondary reason for a cloakroom. It was the place where corporal punishment was administered.

My brother made frequent use of the cloakroom in fulfillment of its secondary purpose, and he applied as much effort in avoiding it as he did deserving it. He hit upon a plan.

In due course, he was making yet another trip to the cloakroom, followed by Sister Mary Marquis de Sade, who was armed with the ever-handy yardstick and a fearful glint in her eye. As she raised the yardstick to apply the first of his well earned forty-minus-one lashes, he dropped to the floor and expelled a scream of mortal pain.

To the other teachers and the janitor and the students, it sounded like he was being disemboweled and his mortal remains were being trampled on by hobnailed boots. All of the above mentioned gathered at the cloakroom to witness his last hour. They saw him writhing in pain and Sr. Mary M. de S. standing over him with her weapon and looking helpless, embarrassed, confused, apologetic, and anxious to explain.

A subsequent conference between Sr. and my parents, armed with some clarifying information from my sister, resulted in the whole incident being satisfactorily resolved.

But that type of discipline, though it may have helped students develop their imaginations and enterprise, very likely accounts for our generation growing up with sadistic tendencies and warped psyches as we now know from the studies of "experts." But, of course, many "experts" disagree.

Getting Bent on Golf

by Father Elstan
October 1988

Almost every weekday at 5 p.m. I drive down County Road 11 on my way to Chaska for evening prayers and supper with the friars at Guardian Angels. As I drive past the Deer Run development, I have one eye on the road and the other surveying the progress of the construction of the golf course.

And I reflect and reminisce. It will soon be the scene of the age old drama of the ecstasy of victory and the agony of defeat. I speak from twenty years of experience as an addict of the game.

Years ago I was lured onto a driving range. I was handed a tee, a driver, and a ball and told to hit the ball toward the markers in the distance.

It seemed so simple; and it was obvious the most distant marker was not nearly far enough away. I mean, that small, hard, resilient ball -- that hard, heavy, wooden club ... well, really!

I called out "fore" -- or "four," I never did know which it was, but the game is played according to unbending rules, and if someone is in danger of being hit by your golf ball, you call out in that fashion. I wanted to warn the people in the next county that they were in imminent danger.

I took a mighty swing, and the ball disappeared -- straight up toward heaven. The people who were in danger were the pilot and passengers of a 747 flying directly overhead -- not those in the next county. When the ball finally landed, it came back to virtually the same place from which it had been launched earlier that day. It had almost burnt up on re-entry into the atmosphere.

But I was hooked. That same day I missed the ball entirely, bent the shaft on the driver when I hit the wrong ball (mother earth), let the club slip out of my hands and fly farther than any of my drives, but I was hooked.

The game is too complex and the subject has too many ramifications to be done justice to in one short article. I think I shall pursue this train of thought in subsequent issues. Watch for further disclosures of my golfing addiction in this space.

The Unconscious Woodpecker

by Father Elstan
November 1988

You were worried in last month's column that you would be subjected to more of the history of my golfing career. And so it shall be. Golfers are like fishermen. Once they corner you, you have to hear their story whether you want to or not.

In the beginning, I was so bad that Fr. Armand, with whom I paired up frequently, became so impatient with my holding up the game looking for a lost ball, flailing away in the sand, pulling half a dozen clubs out of the bag before settling on the wrong one, that he sent me off to a local golf pro for a series of lessons.

That was a big help. I learned that there are 103 different things to remember in the process of bringing the club into contact with the ball and that the omission of one of those things would result in an errant shot. Now I could generally look back after a swing and trace the problem to the thing or things that I had neglected.. Before that I didn't have the vaguest idea what was lacking.

One day I was out with three of the local clergy to our weekly eighteen holes. We came to the 6th hole. I teed up, swung mightily and sent the old Titleist II on its journey down the fairway.

But when it got out about thirty yards, it took a sharp right hand turn and sailed into the top of a tall pine tree. There was a dull thud, and down out of the pine and onto the ground fell an unconscious woodpecker. The ball landed right beside him.

After patiently enduring some very predictable bad humor ("Is that the first time you ever got a birdie on this hole?" ... "You're the only one of us that got a birdie on this hole." ... "Is that the first birdie you ever got?" etc., etc.), I plodded on down the fairway to where the ball and bird were lying.

I was preparing to hit the ball when the woodpecker staggered to his feet, shook himself, and took off, following a rather erratic line and casting a nasty glance back at me as he headed for the wild blue yonder, presumably in search of a medical expert to consult about his roaring migraine and the lump that was emerging through the feathers on his head.

It was a nine hole course, so in doing our eighteen, we eventually came around to the fateful 6th hole again. I bent down to tee up and, when I did, there was a roar as of a mighty wind as birds of all sizes and descriptions bolted out of the trees, shrubs, brush, and grass in the area. I had to endure some more bad humor, but there was general consensus that word gets around swiftly in the bird community.

Sister Twiggy Plays Golf

by Father Elstan
December 1988

It being the Christmas season I should, perhaps, say something about it, but since I've gotten off on the topic of golf in the last two columns I'll continue to pursue that subject and then introduce the Christmas theme at the end.

It is a remarkable phenomenon with golfers, and one that I've never had satisfactorily explained, that after they have taken up the game and made contact with the ball five or six times, they assume they are qualified to offer kindly advice and astute observations to any and all others whom they see afflicted with the same vice.

I, too, fell victim to this assumption and found myself giving helpful hints to people who could come in with a lower score than I, even if they employed one hand -- playing blindfolded -- and used a Ping Pong ball.

But I finally found someone whom I could legitimately instruct. I was stationed in Harbor Springs, Michigan. Fathers Flavius, Tom, and I frequently checked out the various courses in the area.

And frequently the Sisters, out in the school yard with their charges, saw us merrily driving off together, obviously to go golfing. They and the children would always innocently ask: "Where are you going, Fathers?" Our answer was always the same: "We're going on a solemn sick call."

They, the Sisters, frequently adverted to the fact that we were lucky to be able to get out and play golf -- whereas they had to stay home and work, and never got to play golf. This nasty problem had to be corrected.

I told my problem to a local golf course owner, who said he would set aside a whole afternoon, supply the equipment and try not to wince openly as they dug up his tee-off areas and fairways. Nine Sisters responded to the invitation. Father Flavius took three, Father Tom, three, and I, likewise.

In my group was Sister Dianne Marie. Sr. D. was constructed along the lines of the Metrodome. About this time in the history of events, there was a celebrity, from England, I think, who was setting the standard for feminine appearance, who called herself just "Twiggy." She looked like an advertisement for anorexia. She seemed to be put together with toothpicks and matchsticks.

It was only a matter of time before we began to refer to Sister as "Sr. Twiggy Marie." Sr. Twiggy's ignorance of golf and enthusiasm for the game were about equal -- both boundless.

I teed up her ball, handed her a driver, showed her which end of the club to hold in her hand, how to hold it, and pointed at the flag some 410 yards straight ahead and said, "Hit the ball toward that flag." She did, some 250 yards straight, as instructed, at it.

Somewhat shaken, I teed off, and Sr. T. wanted to know why I didn't hit my ball where she hit hers. I explained there were refinements to the game that she would be told about by and by, and that I was placing my drive to allow a better angle of approach to the green with my second shot.

I gave her a five-iron and told her about clubs being built with different angles of loft so she could take a full swing and not worry about going too far. She dropped the ball on the green. When I stopped blinking, I worked my way to the flag.

It was time for Sr. T. to putt. I showed her a putter. With my dissertation on the various clubs being tilted for the right distance and results still fresh in her mind, she walloped the ball across the green, through the rough, and into a neighboring forest. It took her seven strokes to get back to the green. She blamed me.

The rest of that day is not one of my fondest memories. She got better as she went along. After 18 holes she wanted to see the score card, which I reluctantly showed her. She expressed great disappointment: "Oh, you beat me. You've got a bigger score than I have."

After absorbing that for a few minutes, I consoled her with the reminder that it's a complicated game and she couldn't expect to be perfect the first time out. That made her feel much better, the poor dear.

Oh, with regard to Christmas -- a Merry, Peaceful, and Blessed one from St. Victoria's.

A Ball Hits the Left Hind Pocket

by Father Elstan
January 1989

Let's take one last look at the golf scene.

When one has golfed for a length of time, he (or she) inevitably accumulates a store of memories of superb shots, memorable shots, and lucky shots that make up part of his or her golfing experience. In my case, memorable and lucky shots outnumber superb ones by a considerable margin.

In the category of "memorable," the event that comes to mind first is the time I was out with Father Adolph Tillman on a course in Petosky, Michigan. We came to the third hole and he drove off first. He then walked across from the tee-off area and bent over to tie his shoestring. While he was thus distracted and facing away from me, I teed of and shanked the ball in such a pronounced manner that it shot across in front of me and connected with Fr. A.'s left hind pocket.

He rose into the air like a flushed pheasant, employing words and phrases that are not usually associated with one in sacred orders. By the time he landed and had turned around, I was teeing up another ball. He made, what in all honesty I had to admit was, a reasonable inquiry: "Where did that ball come from?" I answered with a question that I thought equally reasonable: "What ball?"

"The one that hit me in the left hind pocket" (or words to that effect).

"Beats me! Must be someone on the other side of that rise coming up the fifth fairway. Now, will you please hold your peace while I get off my drive. Chapter seven, verse ten of the book of golf etiquette states explicitly that you may not talk or make distracting noises when one in your group is addressing his ball. I'll thank you to observe that rule scrupulously."

He dropped his voice, but continued to mumble something about the book of golf etiquette, also saying you are supposed to yell "fore!" when you hit a ball that may endanger someone.

To this day, he does not know where that ball came from, nor do I intend to tell him. It will all be revealed at the last judgment, of course, and I'm not looking forward to it, but, till then, discreet silence, I think.

In the "lucky" category, I remember a number. Notable among them was a time at the country club in Columbus, Nebraska, where Father Armand and I frequently tried our skills, to use the term loosely.

It was a first time out in the spring after a long hard winter, a beautiful day in early April, and there was still a small patch of ice floating around in the middle of the pond that made up most of the distance between the tee-off and the green on the 143-yard, par three, fourth hole.

I got off a big six-iron shot, but the ball hit the patch of ice, bounced up on the shore and rolled within inches of the hole.

In his frustration, Fr. Armand employed a wealth of descriptive vocabulary that rivaled in color and clarity that used by Fr. Adolph in the incident narrated above.

This is getting a bit lengthy, and I had hoped to cover the field in this column, but perhaps a few more incidents that deserve being immortalized in print will appear next month -- if nothing of significance presents itself by then to edge them out.

Till then, may God bless your New Year with grace from His bounty.

Eagle on a Par Five

by Father Elstan
February 1989

Still adhering tenaciously to the golf theme, I would consider no history of great moments in the sport complete that didn't include the story of my 465-yard drive, executed on June 12th, at 9:32 a.m. in 1965.

Four of us clergy from various points on the compass had spent a considerable amount of time -- and money on long distance calls -- arranging to get together for a golfing vacation. The plan, as mapped out by our fearless leader, was to play every course between Omaha and the West Coast and back that we could find in a three-week period of travel.

He, the above-mentioned "leader," had become so engrossed in the planning and research that goes into such a project that we were 250 miles into the Nebraska sand hill country before we discovered he had forgotten his golf clubs. But that's not really germane to the real point.

Our first stop was at Ester Park in the foothills of the Rockies where there is a beautifully hilly course. Hole Number One is 465 yards, slightly downhill, wide and unobstructed, ideal for one who occasionally chooses to employ a pronounced slice.

I teed up, and the old Titleist II was on its journey to the green, 465 yards straight ahead. It traveled well for about 100 yards when an invisible force took over and directed it sharply to the left and deposited it in a mountain stream that flowed parallel to the fairway and directly past the green.

When I got up to the ball, it was still moving along from the force of the flowing water; and it continued to move along till it got to the green, where it washed up on a tuft of grass. I chipped it on and putted out -- an eagle on a par five hole!

My companions made a number of remarks, all of them derogatory, but when it came time to announce scores, they mentioned theirs in subdued tones.

With this historic event recorded, I shall lay to rest the golf motif and go on with some other inspiring topic next month. May Victoria's Deer Run Golf Course give you many hours of recreation and relaxation and enduring memories.

Dance of the Fire Ants

by Father Elstan
March 1989

I know, I know. I promised that last month's column would be the end of the series on the subject of golf, but I have subsequently recalled something that must be recorded if the history of the game is to be complete.

Father Don Wunderlich stopped by one time when I was stationed in Louisiana. It was in April when all the world called to anyone with a drop of sporting blood in his veins to go out on the links and lower his handicap. Accordingly, we made our way to the local municipal course.

The first hole was long and straight, bordered on the left -- or west -- side by dense semi-tropical jungle. As was my custom, I hooked my drive into the lush undergrowth.

Fr. D. and I went into the primeval swamp in search of the ball, swinging our golf clubs like machetes to clear the way. We had struggled a few yards into the tangled vegetation when we both stopped abruptly at a sound like steam escaping from a ruptured pipe.

There in front of us were two cottonmouth snakes, evidently irate at having their solitude disrupted, their mouths open like the back end of a dump truck, and looking for all the world like something out of the Book of the Apocalypse.

We left them to their solitude. We also left a peace offering -- a perfectly good Dunlap II golf ball, two slightly used three-irons (Spaldings), and two sets of widely-spaced tracks. Time and tide have no doubt obliterated the tracks, but it's a safe bet the ball and clubs are still there.

Later that summer, Fr. Tom Cashman stopped by. In a spirit of hospitality I took him out on the golf course. He couldn't believe his great good fortune when he came up to his ball for his second shot on one of the holes, to find it teed up neatly on an ant hill. (Not that he wouldn't have been above improving the lie if it hadn't stopped in such a manner, but this turn of events made it all very legitimate and saved him the problem of struggling with guilt.)

The ant hill mentioned above belonged to a large family of fire ants. These are swift, testy little creatures that are never more testy than when their domestic tranquillity is disturbed. In virtually no time at all after he hit the ball and dug up their happy home in the process, they were up his pants leg, clear up to his neck, inspiring him to perform a dance that was both lively and original. He might just as well not have completed the game after that.

There are dangers inherent in the game of golf other than those posed by the errant shots of other golfers. I cite these examples as a lesson for those who are contemplating taking up the sport as a peaceful pastime

A Knight of the Road

by Father Elstan
April 1989

There is a bonus that we of the cloth enjoy which is perhaps not fully appreciated by us and the layman. We frequently meet some of God's most interesting characters.

Whenever fate deals someone a bad hand and he (usually "he") finds himself adrift on the fringes of society, his bad luck is compensated for by an uncanny instinct for locating and directing his pointing finger at the doorbell of a monastery, friary, rectory, or convent.

Whenever a group of priests congregate -- and they finish solving the problems of the world and the church -- their conversation frequently turns to stories about encounters with these, our less fortunate brothers. I will tell you a few of my favorites.

In 1950, after my ordination, I was sent to Guardian Angels in Chaska. Father Justinian Kugler was the pastor. He had "been through the wars," but in all of his experiences with "knights of the road," he had never become cynical nor very cautious. If we were to trace the origin of P. T. Barnum's famous quote, "There is a sucker born every minute," I firmly believe we would come back to a time when he met Fr. J. K. in person.

One day the doorbell rang. Fr. J. K. answered it. On the other side of the door stood a battered, bandaged, tattered man on crutches. His condition, though sad, was not as sad as his story. Fr. J. K. came into the house, emptied out the petty cash box, the vigil light stands, and Mass stipend fund, and came up with fifty bucks for the poor soul, and sent him on his way with a blessing.

He came back into the house and stood at the window to watch the slow and tortured progress of the man down the sidewalk. When he had hobbled to the spot across from the convent, his health miraculously improved. He straightened up, picked his crutches up off the ground and carried them as he strode firmly toward the doorbell of the Sisters' house.

When Fr. J. K. saw this extraordinary transformation, he picked up the phone and described the scene to the Sister who answered. She met the man at the door with the cold stare of a seasoned fourth grade teacher who had just caught one of her boys shooting spit balls at the girls during religion class.

For the second time that day, the man's health was restored, so completely this time that he was able to tuck his props (crutches) under his arms and run non-stop to parts unknown.

May the joy of the Resurrection be yours this Holy Season wherever you may find yourself in the human parade, whether as one who is healthy, prosperous, and secure, or ailing, hungry, and alone.

The Road Scholar

by Father Elstan
May 1989

I shall have to respond eventually to the "letter to the editor" in the *Gazette* last month from "Moose in Bastrop, LA." I golfed regularly with this man (Father Vincent) in the old days and, by my ineptitude at the game, provided him with periodic guffaws; but to imply, as he did, that I didn't know which end of the club to hold and which end to smite the ball with demands some defense.

But for now, back to the theme introduced in this column last month -- that we in our work as ministers and priests have the good fortune to meet colorful characters on a rather regular basis.

It was about this time of the year and the weather conditions had stimulated rapid growth of the hedge around the front lawn of the monastery at Guardian Angels. Weeds were doing well, too. Also the grass.

Fr. Justinian decided to take the first step to correct the problem. He bought a beautiful rubber-tired wheelbarrow, an electric hedge clipper, a hand clipper, a rake, a hoe, and several other items that were guaranteed to keep our yard in mint condition.

He hadn't decided who was going to use all this equipment until the doorbell rang about that time, and there stood a man whose appearance marked him as one whom the Sisters used to refer to as a "St. Joseph," but whom we frequently called "a road scholar."

With his hat in his hand and his eyes on his shoes (open-toed models), the man informed Fr. J. that it had been a long time since he had eaten, and that he would be willing to work for a meal.

To Fr. J. it seemed like divine intervention, his need and ours complimenting each other so completely. He brought out the wheelbarrow loaded with all the equipment previously mentioned and promised the man that, at the completion of the job, there would be a meal and a ten dollar bill waiting for him.

Fr. J. went off to fix a few sandwiches, a bowl of chili, some fresh fruit and some coffee, and wait for the bell to announce that the work was finished.

After a couple of hours Fr. J. went out to check, but there was nothing to check. Some mysterious force had swallowed up the man, the wheelbarrow, the hedge clippers -- electric and hand operated -- the rake, the hoe, ... and the yard became and remained a tangled mess for the rest of the summer.

The Insulting Handout

by Father Elstan
June 1989

More often than not when someone stops at the door for a handout, his appearance advertises his need before he states it in words. But not always.

The doorbell rang at the rectory of St. Joseph in Bastrop, Louisiana, one day. Upon being granted entrance, the ringer of said bell bounced in with an air of enthusiasm and good will. He was upholstered in suit, shirt, and shoes that said whatever his need, it was certainly not money.

In a conspiratorial whisper he said he wanted to talk to the "head priest." His image lost some of its luster with that remark. However, I saw him across the table to hear his story, a story that outlined another sad tale of man's inhumanity to man.

He had been bilked out of his vast fortune by an unscrupulous business partner, and wasn't it a sad world in which a man can't trust his fellow man. But with his background, experience, and expertise, he was certain he would bounce back, and all he needed from me was a check made out in his name for the paltry sum of $300. There would be untold rewards forthcoming shortly after the transaction.

I put my index finger into my ear, twisted it a few times, and then tapped the side of my head to make sure I was hearing correctly, and asked, "Did you say three hundred dollars?"

"Well," said he, "that would be the minimum. Anything more than that would be accepted, and the return would be proportionately greater, of course."

I figured he had been doing too much reading about the church's vast financial resources and thought she -- the church -- was looking for opportunities to unburden herself of the weight of all that money.

I told the man that three hundred was a bit out of our reach, but I could scrape up THREE dollars for a bowl of soup and a sandwich at the local eatery.

He was insulted. That a person of his stature should be offered a $3 handout was too much, and he stomped off. I swear I saw steam escaping from under his very expensive collar as he passed down the sidewalk and out of my life.

I have been following the news over the succeeding years to see if his name or picture is ever linked with any vast enterprise or captain of industry. So far -- nothing. And I suppose it's all my fault.

St. Victoria Church News

from Editor Sue
July 1989

Father Elstan is on vacation visiting the home of his ancestors in Scotland, as well as other people's ancestors in the British Isles. He may also be golfing over there somewhere. Father Bernardine, who lives in Omaha, has traveled north to take care of St. Victoria, Frieda, and Maude in the interim.

The Rescue of Frieda

by Father Elstan
August 1989

I was about to burden you with an account of my recent trip through the British Isles, but an event has just occurred that calls for immediate attention. Frieda just went to the bosom of Rin Tin Tin Land after having accompanied me through the past seventeen years.

She was born in Meridian, Mississippi, and inherited a list of fancy names that would take a full paragraph to enumerate. A couple in Bastrop, Louisiana, where I was stationed at the time, received her as a wedding anniversary gift from someone -- and they were totally indifferent to her.

They put an ad in the local paper offering her for sale just at the time I was looking for a toy dachshund. I made a quick trip to the address given, plunked down fifty bucks and dug her out from under a wrecked, rusty, 1956 Chevy in their yard, where she was in the company of half a dozen pigs, four or five mangy cats, and a couple of dirt-encrusted little kids. She seemed immediately grateful for the rescue.

I took her home. The Sisters saw us drive into the yard and their hearts went out to her at once. She had more ribs than any puppy I had ever seen. She also had wood ticks, fleas, and other life forms on her whose combined weight exceeded her own.

Sister Colleen took immediate charge, sat down with Frieda on her lap, and spent half an afternoon disposing of her excess baggage. Frieda's gratitude was boundless and she expressed it after each successive removal of a tick or flea.

She became an immediate hit with everybody. Every day, at recess and after school, the kids would come over and play with her. She would be waiting at the door before the bell rang. She would be waiting for Fr. Bernardine when he came home for supper in the evening. She would play with Brother Bill who had been a submarine sailor during the war and didn't know what it meant to be gentle, but Frieda ate it up. She would sit on the lap of Helen, the secretary, as she worked at her desk. She greeted everybody who came to the office, and made their business her own. The word "gregarious" suggests itself when the subject of Frieda comes up.

This will get too long if I exhaust the subject. Maybe I'll continue along this line next month -- more for my own benefit than yours.

Faithful to Rudy

by Father Elstan
September 1989

Perhaps a few final paragraphs on Frieda and then we will let her rest in peace.

In spite of her inauspicious beginnings, as described in last month's column, she grew up with no visible adverse effects to her health or psyche. She got into the normal scrapes and scraps of a puppy in a household. But on one occasion she exceeded the bounds of ordinary exuberant youth.

We were in Louisiana where several clergy would periodically gather for a game of golf. Since it was always hot in Louisiana, after the game, we came to the closest rectory for a tall cool one. On this occasion we were in my rectory in Bastrop.

We were sitting in the recreation room, checking our scores and doling out dimes to those to whom we had lost. I put my Manhattan on the floor next to my chair as we talked. When I reached for the glass it was empty. In a flash my powers of deductive reasoning led to the conclusion why it was empty. Frieda was cowering in the corner of the room with one eye spinning clockwise and the other counterclockwise. Her hind legs weren't working very well. Neither were her front legs.

She always enjoyed chasing a ball. I tested her sobriety by tossing a golf ball down the corridor. She took out after it and ran into the wall. With grim determination, she rose steadily and ran into the other wall. When she finally came to where the ball had stopped, she dropped her head down to pick it up -- and missed it.

The next morning her eyes were the color of a sunset on the desert, and it was apparent she didn't appreciate sudden noises. I believe it was then that she joined AA and stayed with it the rest of her life! In fact, the sight of a bottle with X's on it visibly disturbed her from that time on.

In the course of her childbearing years, Frieda begot ten puppies on four different occasions. All of them were the progeny of Rudy, a dachshund of dubious character. Rudy hung out with a tough gang in back alleys of Bastrop and had survived numerous gang wars and confrontations with irate tomcats.

He had a scar the full length of his long nose, a lip that hung half open and gave him the appearance of a permanent scowl. He had ragged ears, a partially truncated tail and a belligerent glint in his shifty eyes. He looked like one of Al Capone's more high-salaried hit men.

But Frieda thought he was the most handsome fellow that ever came down the pipe -- and I am proud to say she was faithful to him all her life, a fact that deserves complimentary comment in this age of easy virtue and casual commitments.

But almost eighteen years of easy living finally caught up to Frieda, and she had to hand in her dinner pail, leaving her companion, Maude, morose, depressed and inclined to blame me -- for leaving the house with Frieda and coming back without her.

Arriving in London Town

by Father Elstan
October 1989

One of the benefits of taking a long trip is that when you return, folks feel an obligation to listen to your endless and enthusiastic account of the thrills and adventures you experienced. I've cornered just about everybody and now must resort to this expedient to reach the rest of you in regard to my trip through the British Isles in June. So, kindly read on -- patiently.

Eight hours in the air, through the night -- a sleepless night -- left us groggy and cranky when we landed in Gatwick, fifty miles out of London. ("Us" and "we" from now on will refer to my brother Jesse, Fr. Don and me.)

We were in no condition to get a good impression of any place, even if we had landed in the middle of paradise; and I doubt if we would have gotten a good impression of Gatwick under any circumstances.

After getting sorted out by perky, red-clad tour guides with clipboards on their arms and harried expressions on their faces, we were funneled into a bus for the trek to the Barbican Hotel in the middle of London Town. (I remember little of that journey.) But that left us with a lot of time to blow before the regular tour bus was to leave the next A.M. for our highly recommended trek through the United Kingdom. So we took a tour through London.

I remember little of that tour either, except the time spent at the Tower of London. One reason I recall that vividly is because the young lady taking us through those historic regions had the voice and personality of a marine sergeant. Another reason is because I felt a certain link to the Tower (actually there are 24 towers, one more ominous looking than the other), because a number of my ancestors spent their declining years there, having exhibited a degree of disrespect for the Roman law.

Somehow or other we got separated from the group, possibly because we made a conscious effort to put distance between us and "the voice" and possibly because we had all fallen asleep on our feet. At any rate, when we became conscious of our status, we enlisted the cooperation of a series of subjects-of-the-crown to arrive at the departure point of the bus back to the hotel in time.

There is a bright side. All who had been blessed to be in this top sergeant's group were expected to tip her at the end of the tour. When that time came, we were elsewhere.

The next day we started on our 18-day, 3100-mile odyssey through Great Britain. On the first stop out of London -- at some ghastly castle or crumbling cathedral, I don't remember -- something happened that set the tone for the entire trip. We met Rose!

Remember that name. It will occur again and again. But since Rose deserves an entire column, and will get it, I'll save her till next time.

St. Victoria Church News

from Editor Sue
November 1989

Father E. is on a spiritual retreat and the *Gazette* must do without him this month.

Meeting Rose from New Yawk

by Father Elstan
December 1989

Before this column was interrupted by a spiritual retreat I made in October, I had threatened to tell you about Rose, whom we (my brother Jesse, Fr. Don, and I) met on our bus tour of the British Isles.

It was the first stop, after we left London, at some ghastly castle or other of great historical significance, no doubt, surrounded by acres of park land. We were all still in our first fervor, and so went about the tiring business of tramping the whole thing. Our perky tour guide (Ms. Campbell) had told us the exact time to be back at the bus and that no tardiness would be tolerated.

So Jesse and Don and I were hustling back when we noticed this lady from our group who was struggling along a considerable distance behind the rest and losing ground with every step. We dropped back, figuring that if four of us were late for the deadline, they would be less likely to take off without us than if there were only one.

The moment we joined Rose she launched into her life history. She married a war vet who died after they had two children, a son and a daughter (here-in-after referred to as her "dawdda"). She also had a grand dawdda. After telling us that, she mentioned she was from Brooklyn. We would never have guessed it.

She told us about her struggle to keep the family afloat until one happy day when she got hit by a car crossing the street. While she was in the hospital recuperating, she sued the City of "New Yawk," seventeen witnesses, the guy who hit her, and his third cousin in Halifax. The upshot was she could now travel -- financially secure, unhampered by dawddas, sons, grand dawddas, or husbands -- a thing she had always wanted to do.

Throughout this tale of woe, we were losing ground and getting a little nervous. One of the things that slowed her down was a gimpy hip, a consequence of her accident. Another thing was that she had, in the course of her years, overdone the carbohydrates in her diet. No one asked her age (no one dared), but it was somewhere between 55 and 103.

But she did say that she was Jewish, a revelation that came as no surprise since she interspersed her conversation with phrases that were certain tipoffs as to her ethnic origin: "Oi vey!" and "Oi gewalt," etc., complete with appropriate gestures.

Before we got back to the bus, and when the rest of the group was so far ahead they were out of sight, Rose spotted a "loo," the term universally used for "biffy." She veered off toward it, explaining that she had been on tours before and if you are smart you seize every opportunity. There is no "tellink" when the bus will stop again.

While we were waiting for her we discussed the feasibility of sending one of us ahead to tell the tour guide and bus driver that the road was washed out where we were going next or creating some kind of diversionary action till Rose could join us.

But finally Rose emerged from the loo under a full head of steam and picked up her narrative right where she had left off -- never missing a beat.

There is more to say about Rose. She figured large in the trip's enjoyment. Before I go into that next time, I notice that a Jewish high holiday comes up on December 23rd, Hanukkah. To all of you readers of the *Gazette*: "Merry Christmas." To Rose: "Happy Hanukkah."

Rose and Her "Doo Dads"

by Father Elstan
January 1990

Last month we left you with Rose puffing and wheezing at the door of the bus, having gotten there just before its departure time. This performance was to be repeated at each stop of the bus over the next three weeks of the tour.

Her manner of boarding the bus was to enlist the aid of everybody inside and everybody outside -- the one side to pull, the other side to push. Once inside the bus, she would pause in the aisle to thank everybody for their invaluable assistance, then to spot where Fr. Don, or Jesse, or I were sitting and plunk down beside one of us -- regardless of what the prearranged order of seating happened to be. The tour guide quickly adjusted to Rose's independence.

Her manner of exiting the bus became routine as well. She always descended the steps backwards, with the bus driver and tour guide outside prepared to catch her, and the two or three next to her inside holding on and giving her a running report of her progress.

As she gradually lowered herself to the ground she announced her immediate goals -- also a remarkable routine: "First, I'm going to find the nearest 'loo.' Then I'm going to go to that cute little shop we just passed. Then I'm going to have some tea and a bagel, if I can find one, and I'll be back here in plenty of time."

She always succeeded in each of these worthy endeavors -- except to "be back in plenty of time." Her return to the bus after each stop was also something to which we all grew accustomed. She always came back with enough gifts to weigh down three camels and a pack mule, and always turned to whomever was nearest to her to help her carry them onto the bus and store them in the overhead -- and that whether they were willing to help or not. Rose wasn't choosy.

Once the bus was underway Rose would have one of us drag her shopping bags full of "doo dads" down from the rack; and she took each item out, announced the price (always a "bargain"), and disclosed for whom she got it: "This toy sheep is for my grand dawddah. She'll just adoha it. This Irish linen is for my dawddah. She'll adoha it."

Problems presented themselves to Rose as the trip progressed and her loot piled up: "Boys, how am I going to get all this stuff back to New Yawk?" Jesse suggested we throw it all into the Galway Bay and hope it would eventually drift ashore on Coney Island where she could retrieve it. She vetoed that suggestion.

He took a different tack: "Why don't you just stop buying something every time we stop? Think of what will happen to the economy of the United Kingdom when we go home and cut off the flow of American capital."

The financial problems of the Empire were no concern of Rose's; but she did agree, "I've got to stop. I'm not going to buy anything for the rest of the trip." The resolution lasted till our next stop.

I have no idea how she did get it all back to "New Yawk," but I do know this: She involved all the menials in the Barbican Hotel in London, the mechanics, flight attendants and pilots of Northwest Airlines, and a large portion of the population of "New Yawk." And she did get it all back home safely, I am confident.

Rose's Tour Tragedies

by Father Elstan
February 1990

I might entitle this piece: "Several of Rose's Tour Tragedies." I will only recount the most memorable.

Each morning when we sat down to breakfast, the events of her night were recounted to all who would listen. She noted each morning that there was no washcloth in her bathroom. She was right. There never was in anybody's bathroom throughout the whole trip.

If some aggressive American entrepreneur were to convince the citizens of the United Kingdom of the practicality of a washcloth, he could have a monopoly on the trade, snake a quick fortune -- and elevate the level of civilization in Great Britain by a large number of degrees.

But one morning Rose didn't show up for breakfast at all. Several of the ladies on the tour were dispatched to her room to investigate. They appeared at the bus with Rose in tow looking like she was suffering from viscosity and thermal breakdown. It was all narrated to us on the bus.

The narrative started out with "Oi vey!" and proceeded to describe how she had gotten stuck in the bathtub and was just about resigned to its becoming her casket when she popped loose. I can see how it could happen. British bathtubs are deep and narrow -- and so far off the floor they should be equipped with a parachute for when you jump out of them.

Jesse thought it would be a worthwhile financial venture to organize a consortium and sell tickets to the next day's performance. Wiser heads prevailed and an emergency squad of discreet ladies was organized to check her out every day.

One day, at a stop, I was separated from Jesse and Father Don and was wandering around by myself and it got warm. I ducked into a tea shop to get a restorative spot of tea and a biscuit. Here was Rose with a handful of coin-of-the-realm spread out on the table before her, trying to figure out her financial status. I wasn't much help, but a distinguished-looking British citizen at the table next to us detected our problem and came to help.

In the course of the conversation Rose mentioned she was from Brooklyn. To impress us with his knowledge of the terminology currently employed in the colonies, the chap, with a smile breaking through his mustached upper lip, said, "Oh, a Brooklyn broad, hey?"

He shouldn't have said that. The blood of a thousand Old Testament prophets boiled up in Rose, most of it rushing to her face. In terse and graphic phrases she informed him that no one ever called her that and got away with it even if he was the first cousin of the Queen of England!! The poor man, muttering apologies, backed off into the crowd and out of our lives.

Rose and I headed back to the bus -- I listening, she expounding on the ignorance, insolence and presumptuousness of certain subjects of the Crown. When we got back in the bus she had to recount the whole event again. Most of the tour group saw a great deal of humor in it all -- but no one laughed.

Later that day the bus was traveling through a sizable town. Suddenly Jesse said, "Rose, look. But don't take it personally." Across a street in large letters announcing the name of the thoroughfare were the words: "Broad Street." Somehow or other he got away with it. I guess by that time her Jewish blood had settled back into its normal location.

The Longest Name

by Father Elstan
March 1990

We have a long way to go on our tour of the British Isles, so let's get on with it.

On our way to the Welsh border, our bus disgorged us at "Stone Henge," a pile of rock of considerable historic and archeological interest. The authorities have had to put a barrier around Stone Henge because of the propensity of tourists to chip off pieces as souvenirs, and to leave excerpts of deathless prose and soul-stirring poetry written on the stones' surfaces.

We passed through the English Moors, a vast expanse of bogs, usually enshrouded in fog and mist -- the area that inspired Sir Walter Scott's classic, "The Hound of the Baskerville." If Rose, our Jewish companion from "New Yawk" hadn't been snoring so loudly as we drove through this eerie landscape, we might have been able to hear the mournful howl of that famous hound.

For the next many miles we endured an endless series of bombed out cathedrals and crumbling castles, and finally crossed into Wales, an endless series of slag heaps, ewes, rams, and lambs.

By and by, we pulled into Cardiff, the center of Welsh activity. We were about to board our bus the morning we left Cardiff when I mentioned to one of the motel employees that we were going to be in the little town with the long name that day. He grinned and said, "Oh, that would be ...." and he began to rattle off the name. It sounded like a filibuster in the Welsh parliament.

Long before he completed his recitation, we were ushered into the bus and left Cardiff -- on our way to (my apologies to the typist) "Llanfairpwllgwyngllgogerychwyrndrobwllllantysiliogogogoch." The Welsh claim that is the longest name of a town in the world. I've never heard of that claim being contested.

As we drove along, I couldn't help but imagine a scene of someone starting out in the early morning in search of this town and stopping to ask one of the natives for directions. "I say, old chap, can you point the way for me to Llanfairpwllgwyngllgogerychwyrndrobwllllantysiliogogogoch?"

And the reply: "Continue on to Bryngwenllian. Take the first turn around to the left and go on till you see a large (what else?) sign with the name Llanfairpwllgwyngllgogerychwyrndrobwllllantysiliogogogoch, and follow the arrow. After about seventeen kilometers you will see another sign on the outside of town, Llanfairpwllgwyngyllgogerychwyrndrobwllllantysiliogogogoch, announcing the town and your destination. God speed and good evening to ye."

Lest you think that this town's name is the result of a random conglomeration of letters -- or the result of someone's having spilled their alphabet soup -- there is an authentic English translation for it, if you have the time to read it. In civilized language it means: "The Church of Mary in the hollow of the white hazel near the fierce whirlpool and the Church of Tysilio by the red cave."

Whew! Let's get out of here and cross over to Ireland next time.

Rose and Her Cargo

by Father Elstan
April 1990

If you are still with me on my harrowing hegira through the British Isles, we have passed through the large town of Cardiff and the very small towns of Bryngwenllian and Llanfairpwllgwyngyllgogerychwyrndrobwlllantysiliogogoch (you may remember the names) and are now on the Welsh coast, preparing to board a mammoth boat for a four and a half hour trip across the Irish Sea to the Emerald Isle.

The boat deserves some attention. On the bottom floor they stowed a fleet of tour buses, cars, motorcycles, and four- and three-wheelers, and, of course, countless bicycles. Among the other amenities it offered were a huge dining area and (what else?) a gift, knick-knack, souvenir store.

Our Jewish companion, Rose, whom you have met in previous accounts in this column, spun like a tenpenny nail near a large magnet and headed straight for the above-mentioned shop. There she spent most of the trip, much of her cash, and virtually bought them out.

As we approached the Irish shore she began to put on her hopeless look and to implore the aid of God and all her departed Hebrew ancestors to help her transport her cargo to the bus in the basement of the ship. Her ancestors didn't respond too well, but most of our tour group did, getting themselves and her loot to the bus in time. Rose came late, empty-handed, and full of gratitude to her faithful porters. She had taken the opportunity to step in at a loo on her way down to the hold of the ship.

Our next adventure was going through Irish customs, so our first impression of Ireland was a bad one. The officials looked very official -- serious, tough, as if they had been on a diet of raw meat and been studying passages from Dostoyevsky by heart.

Our tour guide had warned us that when we drove through customs and an officer walked through the bus we were not to try any kind of levity with him, and we should try to look as innocent as we possibly could. Rose began to practice her seraphic look. Her success was impressive. By the time our minion of the law walked down the aisle of our bus she could have been mistaken for the twin sister of the archangel Gabriel. Well, after all, she had the biggest stake in not being detained for inspection. If he had chosen to search our baggage for hand grenades and dynamite, by the time he went through all of her spoils we would have been there till the crack of doom.

From the time we drove away from the scowling border guards, our impression of Ireland -- and the Irish -- improved immeasurably. I believe most Irish are born with a smile on their face (a roguish smile), and they keep it there till they die.

Next month I will cite a few examples of just what I mean.

Never Directionless in Dublin Towne

by Father Elstan
May 1990

If you are still with me on our tour of the British Isles, we are on our way to "Dublin's Fair City." Whereas in England we saw innumerable lambs, rams and ewes, and in Wales we saw slag heaps and ewes, rams, and lambs, in Ireland it was rams, lambs, and ewes, and peat bogs and peat bricks as far as the horizon.

Our arrival at the hotel in Dublin coincided with the evening meal. Father Don, Jesse, and I sat down in the attractive dining room in the hotel where Kathleen Brannigan swooped down on us with solicitous service and sparkling conversation.

Before we even had a chance to review the menu we were informed that Kathleen came from County Kerry, of a family of eight, and that she had to leave home and come to work in the big city to help her hardworking and hard pressed dad. And when, in the course of our bantering conversation it came to her attention that Fr. Don and I were Catholic priests, we were immediately placed high on her list of favorite people.

There was in "Dublin Towne" a man named Vincent Coleman, the thirty-eighth cousin twice removed of a man in St. Louis whom Fr. Don knew. He (Fr. Don) was commissioned by his friend to contact this V.C. when he got to Dublin. After our meal Fr. D. pulled out a map of Dublin, spread it out on the table, which Kathleen had swiftly and efficiently cleared, and began to try to find the address on the map.

Presently, the freckled face of Kathleen Brannigan was thrust over our shoulders and she was helping us locate the address. At this juncture, another waitress joined our little discussion group. She looked like she was somebody's kindly aunt. She announced that we couldn't expect much help from Kathleen, as she was from County Kerry and, as everybody knew, people from County Kerry were all a little weak in the head.

While she -- Aunt Bridget -- was running her eyes and finger over the map, Kathleen went off to enlist the aid of the headwaitress, the receptionist, and the hotel manager. After lengthy discussion, our little group of scholars arrived at a unanimous decision on Mr. Coleman's location. Satisfaction and rejoicing reigned supreme. Then they joined forces to give us detailed (and conflicting) instructions on how to get to Mr. Coleman's most swiftly, efficiently, and inexpensively.

We didn't really care that much how to reach Mr. Coleman's home or work place. We had no intention of going to him. We had his phone numbers (home and work) and merely tried to find these two spots on the map out of curiosity, but the goal of the staff at the Dublin hotel was such that we didn't have the heart to interrupt their research -- nor did their constant and happy chatter as they carried on their detective work allow us any opportunity to interrupt them.

That night we established communication with Mr. Coleman on the phone. He arranged to meet us at the hotel the next day. (The tour was stopping in Dublin for two full days.) Promptly, as planned, he popped in, led the way to the bar, and suggested the proper beer for the occasion. He was an authority. His occupation was a bartender in -- not just another pub -- but "the foinest one in all of Dublin Towne, mind ye."

His conversation flowed fast and easily, and after an hour and a half he was compelled to take his leave, but only after having given his assurance that he would shortly be coming to the States, looking us all up, and accepting our promised hospitality.

Giving directions seems to be a favorite pastime of the people in Ireland. It always seems to be a community thing as well. Everybody has to get in on the act. Fr. D., Jesse, and I made it a point, wherever we stopped, to ask someone for directions to a place in the town, whether we cared to find it or not, just to have the experience of enjoying the process.

In one city (I don't remember which one), we stopped two high school girls and asked them for directions to the local church. They went into a huddle to get it straight, then called in the rest of their class who were scattered over an area of a block and a half, dispatched two of their number back to school to get Sister Superior's expert advice and, after a quarter of an hour, we parted company --

they shouting revisions and additions to their original directions, we being grateful, charmed, and thoroughly confused.

In another town we were standing at a corner and behind us loomed a huge stone wall with an opening in it. We asked a man for directions to the local castle. He called in several bystanders to be witnesses to the accuracy of his directions. Then, with his eyes laughing, but his face very serious, he said, "First ye go one block that way. Turn left and proceed another block. Turn left again, and after one block left again ye'll be right in front of it." It was worth it to see his and his conspirators' enjoyment.

He had, of course, directed us right back to where we were. The wall and opening in it were part of the castle. If you're ever in Ireland and things get dull (something that's very unlikely), ask for directions. You'll get directions whether the place is real or imaginary, and whether the one you ask knows how to find the location or not.

Rose, Our Queen of Sheba

by Father Elstan
June 1990

Picking up from last month's account, our conquest of the Irish Free States continues.

A standard stop on the tour is on Galway Bay, where there is a high, steep cliff overlooking the pounding surf. At the base of the cliff on the path leading to the top of it, a middle-aged, fair-skinned, freckle-faced, obviously 100% Irish couple stood with two obviously African nuns.

They introduced the nuns to all who stopped by to meet them, as "our two daughters, Sr. May Aida and Sr. Oprah Winfrey." These introductions were accomplished with a great effort at seriousness. The two nuns played their parts well, wearing smiles that filled their faces from ear to ear with great white teeth. I suspect that, if the truth were known, they blushed throughout the whole episode as well.

The "Ring of Kerry" is a road built by the Romans during their celebrated occupation of the Island. The road completely encircles the county of the same name. Our bus took us the full length of the "Ring of Kerry."

And I have the story that the men of Kerry took a jaundiced view of their uninvited guests exacting tribute from their meager funds and limited possessions; and to express their disapproval, the Kerry lads fell into the habit, on their days off and under cover of fog and darkness, of slipping into the

Roman camp sites and sticking pitchforks into the seat of the pants of the occupants of the camps, and bouncing bricks and bludgeons off their highly polished helmets -- a most exhilarating form of recreation.

After a while this sport began to pall on the Romans who preferred a quiet, orderly existence, so they built a road entirely around the area and raced their chariots up and down the highway between strategically placed watchtowers and checkpoints, and thus effectively contained the high-spirited men of the region.

Way out in the boondocks in County Mayo there is a pub that dates back to the days of the Druids. It is a "must" stop for our tour buses, not only because of the antiquity and atmosphere of the place, but also because there are two ancient Irish men there -- 95 and 98 years old, respectively. They meet the tourists as they pass through the pub and play a duet on a fiddle and a flute. Their hats are on a stool in full view, resting upside down. The implication is obvious.

On the day we passed through, the older of the two had failed to show up, probably having gotten too old to indulge in such frivolity. The other sat in the middle of the pub with his hands resting on the top of his shillelagh stick and his chin resting on the top of his hands. He stared at the wall with the expression of an Irish man who had had a bad day.

As I walked past him I said: "Pat, how are ye?" Without taking his eyes off the wall, or changing his expression, and in a powerful tenor voice, he announced: "I am physically, psychologically, and morally perfect!"

We were in some town somewhere in Ireland and were about to board the bus to continue the tour when we realized Rose wasn't with us. (You may remember Rose from some previous episodes, the New York Jewish lady who managed to keep our group in an uproar for the full three weeks we were together with her trials, tribulations, and tragedies.)

It was getting late. We organized a search party. The ladies were to go into every loo in town, the men into every shop (a very likely spot) and tea room, and several of us to walk up and down as many streets and alleys as we could find.

We were on the point of departing on our mission of mercy when a police siren wailed, bells rang, and lights flashed; and a black Mariah screeched to a halt next to the bus. Within less time than it takes to read it I thought, "Egad! She's socked a cop! She got run over by a car! She insulted the prime minister!" Others drew equally lurid conclusions.

But then we noticed the six members of the constabulary who were with her were all in a jovial mood, and Rose was riding like the Queen of Sheba in the midst of her attendants, laughing with them and looking immensely pleased with herself.

She told us the story on the bus. She had stopped into the loo on her way back to the bus and when she came out turned the wrong way. She became hopelessly lost. She saw this minion of the law and explained her predicament. He took her into the station and explained it all to his fellow cops. They gave her a cup of coffee and tried to figure out together where the bus might be. Finally, they loaded her into the paddy wagon and drove around till they found us. Her final word: "And they were all so charmink and soooo good lookink!"

Next month we'll leave Ireland and head out across Scotland. Hang in there.

One Marmaduke Coghill

by Father Elstan
July 1990

If you have stayed with me so far on my trip through the British Isles, stay for another couple of installments.

This time we headed up into Scotland, the home of my ancestors. In Edinborough we contacted a cousin, Ronald Coghill, who was expecting our call. He picked us up (Jesse, Fr. Don, and me) and took us to his home about 15 miles out of the city to a neat and quite typical Scotch village called "Bridge of Allen."

He led us into his large library. He said he had spent about ten hours a week for the last 37 years researching and tracing down the far-flung and rather numerous members of our family. Virtually the entire library was stocked with books, genealogies, documents, clippings, court records, birth, marriage, and death records, etc., etc., pertaining to the name.

On his large library table he had spread out and opened a number of books that he thought we might be especially interested in. He certainly was right. To cover all his materials would have taken a year. We only had an hour or so, but in that time we were able to note that when the British decided to rid themselves of their excessive number of convicts and politically undesirable elements and shipped them off to Australia, the Coghill name was in high prominence on the passenger list.

A name that caught our eyes from back in the days of Mary, Queen of the Scots, was one Marmaduke Coghill. Perhaps because he was saddled with that name he had to prove something -- perhaps with a name like that he needed the extra protection -- but, whatever the reason, in the course of his earthly sojourn old Marmaduke begat twenty-three children.

Shortly before Marmaduke handed in his dinner pail (an event he must have welcomed), he was knighted by the Crown. Why he was so honored is open to speculation. Was it in recognition of his extraordinary virility or was it because he kept a steady supply of soldiers and sailors flowing into the service of his country?

Further in-depth historical research is needed to determine the answers to these pressing questions. My own theory is that the king figured any one of his subjects who endured a lifetime with a name like Marmaduke deserved more than a few lines in the obituary columns of the *London Times*.

At the house we met Ronald's giant, friendly (thank heavens), golden retriever, "Duke" (what else?), and "George," a little hedgehog that has taken up residence in the hedge on the edge of the property. Hedgehogs are, I'm told, by nature, night people. But George saw the benefit of being on hand for his three squares a day when Ronald served him -- and slept during the night and the heck with nature.

For the rest of the day we drove a hundred and fifty miles through the desolate, beautiful Scottish highlands. During the ride Ronald told us he had been a professional opera singer, but got a degree in engineering in which capacity he had traveled the world and was presently employed by British petroleum offshore drilling.

He had been married and had a grown son. He claimed he fell for a face and figure like Marlene Dietrich's and only after the wedding became aware that she had a disposition like "Good Queen Bess" with a bad headache; and so he paid her well to stay away.

The conversation veered around to politics eventually and on that subject he was eloquent. He classified all "Brits" and most politicians as blighted, bloody blackguards (pronounced "blaggards"), and sniveling scoundrels; and since Maggie Thatcher was both a Brit and a politician she got both barrels.

We wound up at the end of the day back at our hotel in Edinborough where we had supper together and parted with plans to get together again in the years ahead. Ronald is retiring this year, has bought back some land that our family owned back in the days of the Druids, and is building a home there.

He is going to condense all his research into one book, and as his eyes twinkle he says: "By the time I eliminate all those who shouldn't be in print, I'll have it down to the size of a pamphlet." And, "if each member of the family scattered all over the world buys one copy I will die very wealthy indeed."

Rose at Coghill Hall

by Father Elstan
August 1990

Perhaps, with this installment, we can complete the narrative of our tour of Great Britain which was in progress just one year ago.

The bus headed up through the lake country of Scotland: Locherbie, Loch Lohmond, Lochness, and some lesser known "lochs."

Locherbie exudes an atmosphere of dour depression. It's the place where Pan Am Flight 103 was blown out of the sky -- just a few months before we drove through there. Loch Lohmond had the effect of loosening up the vocal chords of all on the tour as we bellowed out in various degrees of discord: "Oh, ye take the high road and I'll take the low road ... "

Lochness, I suspect, is where the Scotsman has gotten his reputation for being wily. All the natives in the area are dedicated to pulling the rest of the world's leg. Ask any of them about the celebrated Lochness Monster and they will certainly make a great effort at being serious as they tell you about the most recent sightings, the latest frightful encounters, and the most up-to-date proof of its existence. Some have difficulty concealing a sly grin as they carry on their discourse.

The tour stopped for a day in York -- just south of the Scottish border. That was most fortunate. York is about 15 or 20 miles from Knarsborough, the location of "Coghill Hall." We had heard a good deal about Coghill Hall from cousin Ronald, when we spent a day with him in our layover in Edinborough. Jesse had gotten a good look at the exterior and the grounds some years before from the window of a tour bus, and now we had the time and opportunity to see it inside and out.

We noted from some rather descriptive words of our friend Rose, that she had no desire to spend a day in York in pursuit of frivolous pleasures, so we invited her to come along. She knocked the dust from her cane and was the first one into the cab. The driver was gregarious, and before we got to Knarsborough, Rose had elicited from him his whole past history -- and he knew where she stood on all the major issues of the day.

We found the Hall with no trouble. It is a huge, three-story stone structure with Grecian columns, built in 1505 and still in perfect condition. It is located on 80 acres of beautiful land, much of which someone had the good sense to turn into an 18-hole golf course. Through the manicured lawn and very near the Hall flows a trout stream. We had to learn more about this place that bore our name.

We knew already that the land had been granted by the English Crown to one of our ancestors back in the Middle Ages, possibly as an expression of gratitude because he slew his quota of Celts, Picts, and Druids. Then the family lost it sometime in the 1700's, most likely because of a conflict of political viewpoints between us and the royal family. But it kept its original name down through the centuries.

We walked through the massive wooden doors and came up to what was some kind of reception desk, presided over by a severe, bespectacled, super-animated spinster who was attempting to look busy by shuffling a stack of papers -- to get them into perfect order.

Jesse walked up to the desk and said, "Er." And she said, "Yeayas!" And Jesse said, "Er," again. And she did her paper shuffling again and said, "Yeayas, may I help you?" And she said it in a tone that made it perfectly clear she had no intention of helping.

But Jesse forged ahead with his mission. "My name is Coghill, and this Hall was built by one of my ancestors, and I'm interested in seeing it and, if possible, getting some information on its history."

Her paper shuffling activities intensified considerably as she pointed out that she certainly couldn't accommodate us as she was entirely too busy.

"Maybe there is a maintenance man or one of the people who work here or someone ..."

"No, I'm afraid not. As you can see we are all very busy." And she tapped her papers into a perfect square again.

He was about to give up when Rose shoved him to one side and me out of the way to the other, then descended on the desk like the hosts of Midian, plunked her cane and both pudgy hands down in front of our paper shuffling friend, and opened fire. (Father Don had long since faded into the woodwork, as remote from the action as possible.) Rose glared into her bespectacled startled eyes and said, "Put those blasted papers away!! Put them away!"

She slid them over to a corner of the desk.

"Now, listen! If I may take a few moments of your valuable time, these boys ('boys,' mind you) have traveled halfway around the world (Rose never hesitated to use exaggeration if it suited her purpose) at great sacrifice and considerable expense to see the home of their ancestors. If that phone works and you know how to use it, blow the dust off the thing and call the manager of this place!"

The shuffler reached for her papers, thought better of it, and picked up the phone. Almost before she had hung it up, an obsequious, little, sandy-haired business-like chap showed up and introduced himself as Magnus McLeod, the manager of the building. He could scarcely have been more cooperative, informative, and helpful, a complete contrast to the major-domo at the reception desk.

As we were leaving, Magnus accompanied us. When we walked past the desk Rose looked at her recently acquired friend as if she were something a non-too-discriminating cat had deposited there and said, "Cheerio, old thing."

"Old thing" was back earning her paycheck by shuffling her papers in place. I would like to have had her job description. It must have listed as obligation #1: "Shuffling papers into neat piles."

Rose and a Hebrew Hug

by Father Elstan
September 1990

In the last installment in this column I promised I would drop the subject of our hegira through the British Isles last summer. I'm not going to keep that promise. I feel compelled to let you in on some of my impressions of some famous locations in England which we visited on the last leg of the tour.

One of those spots was Oxford, the town of and the university of, where the cream of British minds have been molded for generations. Our Hebrew friend -- Rose of Brookline, "New Yawk" -- was impressed by Oxford. Everybody there was dashing hither and thither, some were dashing to and fro, and all looked like they were on a serious and discreet mission. The hallowed halls and the narrow streets were crowded as an anthill. It reminded her of a subway platform in "New Yawk City" during the rush hour.

We moved onto Stratford-on-Avon where one of the hometown boys had made a considerable impact on the literary scene during the golden age of English letters. "William" was his name, of course. We visited the home where he is rumored to have written some of his most impressive stuff. But his inspiration must have come from someplace else. The only thing Bill's home would have inspired anyone to do would be to seek shelter elsewhere.

As we neared London our tour guide announced that there would be a contest when we pulled into town. We were to guess how many miles we had covered on the tour. The one who came closest was to win a statue of a sheep. Rose had just made it clear to the entire group that she didn't want to see another sheep as long as she lived. Guess who won the statue.

The next morning we were all down in the hotel lobby preparing to leave for our proper airport. Rose was in the middle of the lobby, up to her eyebrows in duffel bags and shopping bags, gunny sacks and suitcases -- all bulging with the spoils of her invasion of the United Kingdom. I feel I missed one of life's greatest experiences -- not being present when Rose went through customs at her airport.

She dug herself out from this colossal collection to give Father Don, Jesse, and me a Hebrew hug and demand (not ask, but demand) that we come soon to visit her in "New Yawk." We promised we would, having no intention of ever doing so. But, by golly, this summer we did. Perhaps you would like to hear about it next month.

We Rang Up Rose

by Father Elstan
October 1990

We will give Rose this final bit of space and then go on to more exhalted subjects.

As you may or may not recall, last month we described the emotional scene in the hotel lobby in London as we said "goodby," at which time she gave my brother and me an ultimatum to come to "New Yawk" and see her this summer. "And bring your wife along," she demanded of Jesse.

He and I spent several sessions together during the winter trying to come up with a credible excuse to get out of it, but nothing we thought of would wash with Rose. We bowed to the inevitable, and in June, Jesse, LaVerne, and I flew into the "Big Apple."

As soon as we got settled in our hotel, somewhere in the middle of Manhattan, we rang up Rose. From then on our time was not our own. She had every minute for the next week planned, and there was no changing it.

"Tomorrow you catch the bus at the corner of blank and blank and get off at Duffy's Square. I'll meet you there."

There are over 7,000,000 people in New York and I'm convinced they all meet in Duffy's Square at 11:30 a.m. along with their visitors and tourists. I thought it would be impossible to spot anybody in that mob. Then we saw, about a half block away, a cane sticking up over the crowd. I recognized the weapon and, sure enough, Rose was on the other end of it.

She produced tickets for an off Broadway matinee and handed them out. The play was not only off Broadway. It was off color as well. Rose apologized to LaVerne, but not to Jesse and me, assuming, I expect, that we frequented that kind of entertainment.

After the show we had to cross the street. That may not sound like big news, but in New York it's a major event. It is well to get into the center of the crowd going across so somebody else will be hit first. It is well, too, to commend your soul to God before attempting the hazardous passage.

A city bus pulled up and stopped six inches across the pedestrian line right where Rose was standing. Everyone else stepped around the bus and went on. Not Rose. She stood there and beat on the front of the vehicle until it backed up six inches -- and then went on.

One day Rose had her son-in-law pick us up early in the morning. He had in his earlier years been a taxi and limousine driver in the city. He was gregarious, well versed in New York lore, and a superb driver.

About 8 p.m. he dropped us off at Rose's apartment where she had spent all day preparing a Kosher meal. Well, friends and neighbors, if I had been born a Hebrew and been bound to eat Kosher, I swear I'd have become a Christian real fast. LaVerne took all of her recipes down -- and I hope she threw them away as soon as she got home. The spread of Christianity in the early days of the Church is ascribed to the working of the Holy Spirit. I believe Kosher food deserves some of the credit as well.

Rose is going to go to Los Angeles in November for the birth of twin grandchildren. She threatens to come through Minnesota on her way home. I mention this by way of warning.

She has some reservations about being trampled to death in a buffalo stampede or being ambushed by Indians, but as long as she can swing her cane, she feels relatively secure. I hope she makes it.

Taunting Tautology

by Father Elstan
November 1990

Several months ago a long line of ancient automobiles drove down County Road #11. The costumes of the cars' pilots, and their passengers, conformed to the era of those vintage vehicles.

The next day Tony Aretz was in the rectory and I asked him, "Did you see those 'old antiques' that drove past here yesterday?" I was referring to the cars, not their occupants, of course.

As Tony picked up on the subject, I was conscious of a nagging sensation that I had said something wrong. Suddenly it hit me -- "old antiques." What an obvious redundancy! Is it possible to have a "new antique"? Wouldn't an antique virtually lose its value if it weren't old? "Old antique," forsooth.

But the errors do creep into our speech, don't they? One of our old (antique) friars gloried in spotting them -- and enjoying them. One day he flipped on the TV and there was a tele-evangelist. He had a Bible in one hand, a fist in the other, and an ever-so-obvious wig on; and he bounded from one end of the stage to the other like a Chinese acrobat as he bewailed the presence of "godless atheists" in our society. Presumably he could tolerate, but barely, those who were merely "godless," and he could probably moderate his wrath against those who were first "atheists," but "godless atheists" stirred him beyond control.

Between him, the Good Book, and "Cheesus," this scourge that was rending the fabric of our civilization would be eliminated forever; and anyone who sent him a generous contribution would be partners in the crusade to defeat "atheistic godlessness."

The field of athletic endeavors adds to our rich linguistic heritage some very creative redundancies. One who was being interviewed a few nights ago gave God thanks that He had "gifted us athletes athletically." How's that again?

And how many coaches are successful because they emphasize the "basic fundamentals" of the game? Merely to stress the fundamentals would hardly cut it, and to insist on their players knowing and exercising the basics would be only half of what's needed; but when they have mastered the "basic fundamentals" (or even the fundamental basics), they can justly anticipate a successful season.

Another intellectual giant, when asked during an interview how he prepared for the big game, became eloquent and gave us the benefit of his sagacious advice. He said he prepared physically by physical exercise, he got his emotional feelings under control, and he thought mentally about what he had to do. There you are, folks! Straight from the oral mouth of our star left tackle.

One of these athletes (who had been gifted athletically) was on vacation in Mexico. His coach was on a fishing trip in Alaska. He wanted to get in touch with his coach so he called him -- "by telephone, long distance." That's where he made his mistake. He should have called him short distance and saved the extra charge. But I'm glad he clarified that he had called by telephone or we would have gone through life thinking he had called him by shortwave radio or contacted him by mental telepathy.

So, may I "reiterate again", unless we guard our speech carefully, we will fall into these "tautological redundancies" ... "and et cetera."

Take Turkeys, Please!

by Father Elstan
December 1990

With Thanksgiving and Christmas and New Year the topics of the day, we see turkeys and chickens getting a lot of favorable press. Upside down on a platter and properly cooked, I suppose they deserve some sort of recognition. But when they appear thus at their ultimate destiny, we readily forget that on their journey to fulfilling their life's purpose, they cause us no end of consternation.

Take turkeys, for instance. Those who raise turkeys will readily admit that someone has to do their thinking for them. They (the birds), if ever they won a blue ribbon at the county fair, didn't do it by being star pupils.

And their disposition isn't all that great either. One of my first childhood memories is of picking up a turkey chick -- with the best of intentions and almost altruistic motives -- and the chick's mother landing on my head with an ear-splitting yodel. She attempted to do me in with fang, feet, and feathers, and would have succeeded if my mother hadn't belabored her with a sturdy broom.

As for appearance -- well, I ask you! There is probably little that could scare an alley cat away from a fish carcass, but I suggest the handsomest turkey that ever strutted across a barn yard could scare it by merely appearing on the scene.

It would seem that with the passage of time, my aversion to these foul would abate to some degree, but that's not the case. The older I get the more my neck takes on the appearance of that of a turkey's, and I don't want to have anything in common with them at all.

And how about chickens? My brother and I developed an abiding prejudice against these creatures since the first time we had to clean out their house on a hot day in July. From that time on we were alert to every aspect of chicken behavior that could be justly criticized. We noted that many of the qualities of fallen human nature that are disgusting are most highly detectable in the chicken yard.

What is more pompous than a young rooster trying to crow for the first time? He sounds like he swallowed a golf ball, but he acts like his effort should be recorded in history and be immortalized in song and story. Unaware that the rest of the farmyard fauna are laughing their heads off at him, he goes ahead and makes an ass of himself again -- and again.

As for greed, can anyone exceed that of a chicken? My brother and I used to capitalize on this reprehensible quality of theirs by tossing a lighted cigarette butt into their midst. The most depraved of the lot always got there first and spent the next two weeks with a burnt beak and a seared esophagus. (Our parents stopped us short of tossing a firecracker to them.)

Another ploy we used to teach good manners was to heat a piece of gum and toss it to them. But they never learned. In intelligence they were right down there with the turkeys -- in appearance, too, for that matter.

And, of course, the old rooster's excessive zeal in making sure no egg ever came down the pipe that was unfertilized is legendary. We frequently observed and commented on this dark side of their character as well.

So, friends, enjoy your holiday meal, and reflect that you are removing one more bad example to our children, one more blot on nature's fair face as you dig into the carcass of your turkey or chicken. Happy Thanksgiving, Merry Christmas, Happy New Year.

Virtues of the Horse

by Father Elstan
January 1991

In this space last month, a definitive study of the morals, manners, and appearance of chickens and turkeys was presented. They were found deficient in all three categories.

Let us go on to explore the virtues of the horse. They have very few to be explored. Historians, of course, in their shallow way, extol the appearance of the horse, which, it must be conceded, is striking and majestic.

But, when you look beneath the surface, you find an animal whose brain would serve better in the conducting of the affairs of an earthworm. Where would the horses of song and story be -- for instance, the Lone Ranger's "Silver," the mounts of the Cossacks, and the hoards of Ganghis Khan, those involved in the Charge of the Light Brigade, the Texas Ranger mounts, and those of the Royal Mounted Police -- if it had not been for a superior intelligence guiding their course and destiny? Running in the wrong direction, I dare say!

As for the horse's manners, they are virtually non-existent, as anyone who has ridden behind one on a plow, cultivator, or buggy will readily attest to.

A case in point, which also affirms my contention that true and complete history is rarely written, is hereby offered. So often the recorder of events leaves out significant facts and subtle occurrences that add color and meaning to the narrative.

There was an equestrian review before the members of England's royal family some years ago. It was a magnificent affair. The nobility was properly seated in the reviewing stand, properly attired, and wearing their proper expressions.

First a group of marchers paraded past, followed by floats and bands; and then came the beautifully decked-out horses and their mounts. The most eye-catching item in the entire parade was a pure white stallion with jeweled bridle, richly finished saddle, and streamers attached to both. On board, and carefully selected by the committee, was a pink-cheeked maiden attired in pink satin and wearing an expression of innocence and genteel charm -- the very cream of British womanhood.

She stopped her steed directly in front of Her Royal Highness, the Queen of the Empire.

The morning before this historic event, the horse had dined on some forage that, when mixed with digestive juices of his stomach, produced an unusual amount of methane. As the day wore on, the pressure built up. This rude beast chose that very moment to release the pressure with a thunderous blast that echoed down Upton Street, up Downing Street, across the Strand, and rocked boats and barges on the River Thames.

One citizen in the multitude said, "Egad." Another remarked, "Dash it all!" One went so far as to declare, "Not cricket, you know!" And a less cultured chap, probably in town for the occasion from a remote rural area, slapped his hand to his hat and exclaimed, "Gor-blimey!" Older people present glanced up at the sky with apprehension, anticipating a repeat of the unpleasantness they had with Huns in '41. ("Dashed nuisance, you know.")

Then a reverent hush fell over the assembled multitude as all eyes turned toward Her Royal Highness. They wished to catch her reaction to this ghastly and rude beast's performance. The Queen remained expressionless, serene, and regal.

The poor girl riding the horse, however, was blushing crimson and, in a confused stutter, attempted to apologize. "Oh! Your Majesty! I'm so sorry. That should never have happened. It won't ever happen again. Oh! Your Royal Highness, oh, my!"

The Queen said, "You shouldn't have apologized, dearie. I thought it was the bloomin' 'orse!"

So much for horses' mental acumen and culture.

The Indomitable Hog

by Father Elstan
February 1991

Before we depart from the subject of denizens of the barnyard (you may recall we have recently done an in-depth study of chickens, turkeys, and horses in this space), something must be said about pigs.

Most authors approach this field with a jaundiced eye and deep-seated prejudices. I, on the other hand, find much to admire in the oft-maligned swine. I might interject here that one of those who entertained an unreasonable bigotry regarding pigs was my mother. She had a pathological aversion to dirt, foul odors, and bad table manners, and imagined she detected a close connection between these things and the noble swine. She also, therefore, explained my brother's and my happy relation with hogs by the observation that we had so much in common.

But my brother and I looked beyond these superficial elements and saw in pigs an indomitable spirit and a resourceful and ingenious mind, and we admired them for it.

For example, we strung an electric fence around the hog yard on one occasion. An old sow, who looked like she had never heard of low calorie diets and Lenten fasts, nudged an ear of corn under the wire and in the process of retrieving came into contact with the charged strand.

Can you see that happening to a cow? She would create a stampede. Or a horse? It would light out on a dead run for no particular destination and keep running till it came to a barrier of some kind. Or a sheep, if he got his nose on the wire? He wouldn't be able to figure out what was happening, nor how to correct it, and just lie down and expire.

Not your pig! That old gal just backed off a few steps, scolded the fence in a an ear-splitting soprano voice, and walked back and bit the wire. De ja vu! Then she went down the wire from there about six feet and repeated the performance -- and she kept it up till she had completed the entire circumference of the hog yard. What an indomitable spirit!

On one occasion my brother and I took our high-powered Daisy B.B. gun up to the hayloft to shoot sparrows. We looked out of the big barn window and saw a young hog down below, dining on a cob of corn. My brother had the gun, and when he was in charge of that lethal weapon he generally came up with some kind of unacceptable scheme.

The circumstances now suggested that he shoot the corncob out of the pig's mouth and observe his perplexed reaction. The pellet missed the target and caught our hero on the fleshy part of his snout. He uttered a number of vulgarities, retreated (walked, mind you, not ran) a few paces, then stopped, turned around and walked toward the corncob.

He stopped a few feet short of the corn and stood and contemplated it with an indignant and baffled expression on his youthful face. Finally he strode off to meditate on what happened -- at a safe distance. It was two weeks before he again returned to eating corn-on-the-cob.

With regard to the resourcefulness of swine -- it was my brother's and my lot to carry the slop (I wish there were a more refined word for it, like "liquid nourishment") to the pigs. The trough was one of those that protruded through the board fence where you could pour the repast and not be in danger of being trampled to death by the hungry hoard.

One of the citizens of the above mentioned "hoard" was a member who had been shortchanged in the department of size and sinew -- the undisputed runt of the herd. While the others ate, he had to stand back and watch.

But one day we saw him outside of the fence eating out of the part of the trough that stuck through. We caught him and threw him back and discussed how he had gotten out. The fence was virtually airtight and high enough to contain a kangaroo. The next day we watched.

When the other members of his community bunched up next to the fence, he simply stepped up on their backs, over the top board and dropped down on the other side where he dined in splendid solitude. We admired his enterprise so much we left him get away with it from then on, and eventually he caught up with and surpassed his peers in size and strength.

My admiration for pigs is such that I sometimes consider adopting Hebrew dietary laws.

The Language of Eye and Tail

by Father Elstan
March 1991

There are, I believe, very few in the civilized world -- and probably only a few in the uncivilized world -- who have not heard something about St. Francis of Assisi.

He lived in a century that is outstanding in the world's history for having produced some of our most eminent saints, scholars, poets, and sinners. There are those who refer to that era as the "13th, The Greatest of Centuries."

Even though he lived at a time that begat such an extraordinary group, he stands out most prominently. As a saint he arrived at such a degree of innocence and integrity that his contemporaries and biographers claim he was virtually in the same condition of joy and peace and oneness with the rest of creation that his existence approximated that of our first parents before the snake put in his appearance.

As a poet he saw deeper into reality, and saw it from a different perspective than even most poets of unusual talent. As a scholar his formal learning was limited, but he had a firmer grip on truth than most with PhD's, M.A.'s and S.O.S.'s and E.T.C.'s behind their names.

As a sinner he won rather high marks, too, until he was thrown into the slammer when he was about twenty years old. He came out of that and began his journey to sanctity, at which he ultimately arrived -- to a degree that many think has never been matched.

One of the manifestations of his arrival at an "Eden-like" existence was the remarkable rapport that prevailed between him and the animal kingdom, wild and otherwise. From that aspect of his life there have come down to us, via his contemporaries and geographers, some rather amazing narratives. One such is usually referred as "The Wolf of Gubbio" story.

There was this one-horse town named Gubbio. Most of the inhabitants were shepherds. On the edge of town was a forest. In the forest there lived a rapacious wolf.

On frequent occasions the above mentioned wolf crept out of the woods and stole off with a sheep -- to dine on rack of lamb and mutton chops. The villagers complained to St. Francis. The following is how I picture the unfolding of the story of "The Wolf of Gubbio," and St. Francis had the total trust of all animals.

St. Francis walked into the town singing one of the top twenty on the contemporary charts -- "Sorento," "Isle of Capri," "O Solo Mio." He was usually singing or panhandling.

The citizens of Gubbio complained to him about the wolf decimating their flocks. Francis told them, "Donna you worry. I'm-a feex it for you."

He walked out to the edge of the woods and called out, "Hey, you, Wolf of Gubbio! You comma here. We needa to talk!"

The wolf heard, picked up his ears, and began to slink out toward the direction of the voice. He was good at slinking. He had been taught by his mother how to slink, and he had practiced a lot of slinking since he was a puppy, especially when he slunk up on the flocks of sheep in the fields around the edge of the forest. So he slunk now, because he had noted an edge in the tone of St. Francis' voice.

Finally he emerged from the woods and approached St. Francis. Francis got down to the point without preamble. "Hey, you sommana bee -- er -- she wolf. How comma you eata da sheep of the nice-a people of Gubbio? You cutta dat out!"

The wolf responded (St. Francis understood the language of eye and tail), "I'm-a hungry. I'm-a gotta eat!"

"You no gotta eat sheep!"

"Yes, I do. Da people have-a kill all the rabbits and squirrels."

St. Francis saw the justice of the complaint but missed the point. "I'm-a tella you what. You no eata da sheep, the people no take-a da pot-a shots at you no more!"

"No good. I'm-a still be hungry."

"Hmmm. You right. Hmmm. I'm-a got it! I talk-a da people of Gubbio into putting a meal on the edge of the woods for you every day. You no eata da sheep. O.K.?"

"How I know they keep-a they word?"

"Hey, you beega shot wolf! I'm-a St. Francis. Would I lie to you? We make-a da-deal. We put it on paper. One-a copy for theem. One-a for you. O.K.?"

"O.K."

"So shake-a da hand -- er, paw -- er -- Shake on-a dat."

They shake. St. Francis looks at the sundial on his wrist. "I'll-a be back in-a one hour. Donna go away."

He returned in one hour with an agreement signed by the mayor of the municipality of Gubbio and his councilmen and stamped with the official seal.

The people agreed to have five containers in each household -- one for scrap paper, one for plastic containers, one for tin cans, one for glass bottles, and an extra one for table scraps to provide a daily meal for the Wolf of Gubbio. The wolf read the agreement and put his paw print on the documents.

And, to this day, the progeny of the people of Gubbio abide by the agreement, as do the offspring of the wolf. And St. Francis keeps a sharp eye on both parties to the agreement.

My Brother's Wedding Day

by Father Elstan
April 1991

To most, this is the season of spring. To members of the cloth, it is the beginning of the "wedding season."

I'll bet you lay folks thought that when we of the clergy congregate we discuss the transcendental qualities of being and the eschatological implications of the philosophy of Plato. Of course we do. (Yeah, right!)

But when we've exhausted those and similar subjects, inevitably someone points out that everybody wants to get married at once at this time -- and narrations of past weddings fill up the conversation.

The first was the worst in my experience. I had just been ordained and sent to Chaska when the news of my brother's impending wedding came across the news wires. I was asked to officiate.

The fatal day arrived. The church (St. John's in Jordan) was loaded with an assortment of relatives and friends, some of which r's and f's were loaded, too.

In the front benches sat my mother with the rest of her brood and the bride's nearest and dearest. All in all, it was a scene calculated to strike terror into the heart of the most intrepid wedding officiator.

But all went smoothly. I didn't get my vestments on backwards; the choir carried on professionally; all present wore their best expressions of reverence and attention. I got through the initial questions without becoming tongue-tied: "Have you come here freely, etc., etc." -- "We have."

"Will you love and honor each other, etc., etc."

"We will."

"Will you accept children lovingly from God? Etc., etc.?"

"We will."

It was a piece of cake. Why had I been as nervous as an alley cat in a strange neighborhood? We proceeded with jaunty confidence.

"Do you ..." At this juncture the old gray matter ceased to function. Well, not entirely. Nicknames from the past presented themselves to me in profusion, none of which would be proper to use in church. I could not think of his real name.

But my brother is one who is always willing to help his fellow man when he is in need. His generous nature asserted itself here. In a ringing, penetrating tenor he said, "Jesse, you idiot!"

My first reaction was to repeat: "Do you, Jesse, you idiot, ... etc." However, having been schooled for many years in the seminary in discipline and self-restraint, I cleaned it up and went on with the rest of the ceremony without incident.

Let this be a lesson to you. Don't ever officiate at a wedding without having in a highly visible place, printed in large, legible letters the name of the two combatants. I have followed this rule religiously for, lo, these many years, with satisfactory results.

The Bride Melted

by Father Elstan
May 1991

At every wedding (continuing the theme introduced in this column last month), disaster, like the devil, prowls about seeking whom it may devour; and not infrequently it finds someone to whom it does just that.

I'll long remember this wedding I had in a neighboring town years ago. It was incredibly hot. It was even more incredibly muggy. The bridal party steamed up the middle aisle, took their places, and the ordeal began.

We had just finished the ring ceremony when the bride melted out onto the floor like she had been poured from a bucket. This was a girl who had done herself proud during her lifetime with the carbohydrates and starchy foods. For her wedding she had herself upholstered in yards of slippery material.

The men in the group tried to pick her up. She slid through their hands and arms like a bowl of weak Jello. But finally one of the men, applying a different law of physics, hooked his arms under hers and drug her off across the sanctuary -- destiny unknown -- her feet bobbing across the carpet in random fashion.

While he was applying life-sustaining cool water to her fevered brow, I asked one of the servers to bring a chair and place it where she could sit down when she rejoined our little party. I asked the wrong server. With perhaps a half dozen suitable chairs to choose from, his selection rested on one of those little square stools that are sometimes used to place flower pots on.

Eventually our heroine made her grand entry -- her second of the day -- and plunked down on the above mentioned stool. Her bulk and her flowing gown obscured all evidence of a stool, and the resulting appearance was nothing less than ludicrous.

I am told no photographs taken during the rest of that wedding have been preserved for posterity. It's a shame, really. What interesting questions they would have inspired from her future children and grandchildren.

Imaginary Dandruff

by Father Elstan
June 1991

Were someone to look deeply into the history of "Murphy's Law," they would inevitably arrive at weddings as being responsible for its formulation. For example, in 1959 I was stationed in St. Paul -- Sacred Heart Church -- at 6th and Arcade, the two busiest streets on the east side.

There was a wedding on a warm summer Saturday afternoon. The groom had selected for his best man a lad who was deeply aware of his monumental responsibilities. He assumed the mental attitude that the smooth operation of this entire celebration fell on his unworthy shoulders.

Before the wedding he brushed imaginary dandruff off of his own coat and those of the other male attendants a half dozen times, flicked spots off of his own highly shined shoes and those of his underlings, checked his watch about every third tick, questioned whether the candles were standing perfectly upright, glanced to the back of the church about forty-five times before the wedding started to see if the girls were ready to march up the aisle, and, in general, made an unbearable pest of himself with his unflinching devotion to his duties.

The wedding started on time and without a hitch, thanks to his having checked out every detail.

By and by we arrived at the ring ceremony.

At that point I always hold out a dish of some description to the best man, into which he drops the rings. I did so now, and he dutifully reached into his pocket for them, and his expression changed in an instant from one of serious confidence to one of mortal terror.

Gone were the concerns about dandruff on his shoulders, dust on his shoes, and candles being straight. An item of more immediate consideration replaced these worries. The rings were not there.

He quickly tried his other pockets -- pants, coat, shirt -- and pants cuffs. No rings. Then he went through the entire routine again … and then again. It became a regular routine.

Finally I suggested we go on with the wedding and we would deal with it all later, since rings were not essential to the validity of the marriage. As the wedding progressed he went through all of his pockets several more times, as he poured out pails full of perspiration.

After the wedding I was walking along outside toward the front of the church to greet the couple and assure them that they were committed for life in spite of the absence of rings, when a young man stopped me and asked, "Do you

FROM
THE
EDITOR'S
ALBUM

Father Elstan Coghill, OFM

After ordination in 1949, Father's first assignment was Guardian Angels in Chaska, Minnesota, where he was the assistant pastor -- and adviser for the high school's yearbook staff.

Father's last parish before retirement in 1996 was St. Victoria in Victoria, Minn. He arrived with Frieda and departed with Maude.

Fellow Franciscans

Visiting in Victoria in 1993, Father Bernardine (left), now in Omaha, Nebraska, and Fr. E. were stationed together in Chaska and in Bastrop, Louisiana.

Classmates met in Victoria for a reunion in 1990. (l-r): Fr. Donnard Paulus, Fr. E., Fr. John McManamon, Fr. John Ostediek, Fr. Kennan Dulzer, Fr. Peter Nolascus Kingery, Fr. Titus Ludes. Buried at St. Victoria is classmate, Fr. Louis Diethelm.

Right on Cue

Ready for a strike, Fr. E. introduces bowling to students from Guardian Angels. Photo taken in the early '50's.

Eye on the cue ball, Fr. E. competes with the editor's dad in May, 1996, at the Claeys farm in Ghent, Minnesota.

Right Hand Man

It was a teaching occasion at Guardian Angels School. Students are (l-r): Bonnie (Tschimperle) Riegert, Juane (Salden) Hesse, and Marlene (Pierson) Workman.

The occasion was Father's birthday in 1995. The Victoria ladies are (l-r): Germaine Jesberg, Mary Moore, Julianne Wartman, Mary Meuwissen, Editor Sue, Fr. E.

At St. Victoria

In the spirit of St. Francis of Assisi, Fr. E. initiated and commandeered an annual Blessing of the Animals at St. Victoria. Photo taken in October, 1994.

First Communicants and Fr. E. pray and sing at the altar of the St. Victoria Catholic Church in May of 1996.

The Ecumenical Priest

After becoming acquainted in 1989 on a trip to the British Isles, Jewish friend Rose Chaskes from Brooklyn, New York, visited Fr. E. in Victoria in 1993.

Partaking of a pastoral lunch at the Victoria House in 1993 (l-r): Fr. E., Pastor Bob Johnson (Holy Cross Lutheran), Pastor Frank Jones (Lake Auburn Moravian), and Pastor Doug Roper (Minnewashta Community Church).

Pals

Father Elstan flew to Alamo, Texas, in January of 1996 with the editor and her husband to visit her mom and dad. (L-r): Joe Claeys, Fr. E., Betty Ann Claeys, Allan Orsen.

Victoria's retired postmaster met Father Elstan and friends for lunch at the Victoria House in April, 1996. (L-r): Al Folden, who lives in Apple Valley, Minnesota, Fr. E., Mary Meuwissen, Julianne Wartman (seated), and Editor Sue.

More Pals

Elsa Grace, infant daughter of Paul and Caroline Swanson, receives attention from her pastor. Caroline is the choir director at St. Victoria. April, 1996.

Maude in November of 1994 with her companion, Father Elstan, whose funny bone gets tickled easily.

Life is . . .

In their younger days, these brothers were known as Jesse and James Coghill.
Fr. E. celebrates his birthday here with Jesse in 1994.

Jim and Barb Larkin, friends from St. Hubert's in Chanhassen, Minnesota, came to
help celebrate Fr. E.'s 73rd birthday in August of 1995.

. . . a Celebration

Camaraderie at the Island View Country Club in Waconia, Minnesota, in February of '96. (L-r): Al Orsen, Germaine Jesberg, Fr. E., Art James, David Willadsen, Al Lehner.

Fr. E. and Leota Fiebelkorn, the cook at the Chaska Friary for many years, watch the editor and friend Kathy Kraemer arm wrestle at the kitchen counter, where Father moved for his evening meals when the Friary closed.

Family Gatherings

The family of St. Victoria Choir Members and Fr. E. gathered at the editor's home for the occasion of a baby shower for Elsa Grace Swanson. April, 1996

The editor's family enjoys a first taste of spring in May, 1996. That's son Nick, husband Allan, Fr. E., Sue, and daughter Jenny.

think these might belong to that bride and groom?" He held two wedding rings in his hand.

"Where on earth," I inquired, "did you find those?"

"On the church steps," said he.

I snatched them up, confronted the wedding party, assembled them in proper order on the sidewalk at the foot of the church steps, and supplied the ceremony that was so glaringly missing in church.

It seems that the best man, in checking out everything before the wedding, had reached into his pocket to be sure his keys were there. He took them out to inspect them -- I suppose to be sure they were in working order -- and in the act of pulling them out of his pocket had inadvertently pulled the rings as well, which dropped down on the church steps.

I pointed out in the beginning that the address where this historic event took place was at the well-traveled juncture of 6th and Arcade Streets. It was being well-traveled that day; and the sight of a wedding taking place outside of the church resulted in several near accidents, and undoubtedly endless speculation.

"Harvey! Do you think the church caught on fire during the ceremony?"

"Do you think the Catholic Church doesn't allow certain marriages inside the building anymore?"

"They must have forgotten to say their vows in church."

"I wonder who planned that wedding?"

"The Catholic Church is getting farther out all the time."

And so on.

Hoopla in the Heat

by Father Elstan
July 1991

It is still the middle of the wedding season and so, therefore, appropriate to discuss weddings of the past.

Have you ever been in Nebraska in July? Mark Twain was there on one occasion and he gave a vivid description of the heat. He claimed he saw a coyote chasing a jackrabbit -- and both of them were walking.

It was like that when a couple chose a day in July for their wedding. It was always a day that "broke all previous records" for high readings and humidity.

And so it was on this fateful day when I was stationed there and had to officiate at a wedding on a steaming Saturday afternoon. This event happened in the days when air conditioning in a church was more the exception than the rule. Our church favored the "majority opinion."

To make the event more bearable for the sweating gentlemen and perspiring ladies, we arranged, in strategic locations, several huge and high-powered fans, all of them turned on "high."

The wedding began with the usual sedate procession down the aisle, the men all serious and proper in their tuxedoes, the ladies all self-conscious in their cumbersome hoop skirts.

They lined up in place at the sanctuary steps, and had no sooner done so when the very impressive gale emanating from the fans came into contact with the hoop skirts, to which we have previously alluded, and tossed them toward the ceiling.

I am told there is a place of entertainment in Paris called the "Follies Bergere," where the emphasis is on a plethora of raucous shouting in conjunction with a dearth of modesty. For all practical purposes, the congregation might just as well have been in Paris, France, at the Follies Bergere.

We proceeded with the wedding without the cooling comfort of the fans, choosing that procedure as the lesser of two evils.

It is my sincere hope that the photographer for this event had the discretion to destroy any and all films of that phase of the wedding. What would be gained by having a permanent record of the unfortunate ladies' embarrassment, and a continual occasion for uncalled-for remarks from those who witnessed the fiasco?

The Parking Lot Pilgrimage

by Father Elstan
August 1991

Say, did you go out to the U. S. Open at Hazeltine last month?

I did. I had several tickets and I gave one for Tuesday's practice round to Father Conran. He drove my car. When we parked he carefully marked the location. I took a vague reading on the spot.

We walked to the scene of action and were contributing our quota of "oohs and aaahs" as we watched the "dramatis personae" drive, chip, and putt with disgusting accuracy, when we met a friend of Father Conran's with whom he golfs occasionally.

The three of us continued to hustle up and down the hills of Hazeltine, until about 2:30 p.m., when the thought of roosting permanently on one of the grandstands presented to me a much more exciting possibility than chasing a gang of overqualified golf pros around the course.

I asked Fr. C. if he would take me home and he could come back for the rest of the day. His friend suggested he could bring Fr. C. home and I could take my car and go back. So agreed.

I struck out for the spot where we had parked. When I got there, there was a pickup truck in its place. I looked around for a car with a white ribbon on the antenna. There were 7,000 cars with white ribbons on their antennas.

My next move was to walk among the sea of cars until mine showed up. It never did.

When I had walked my feet down to bloody stumps, I sat down on the bumper of a car to contemplate the plight of the Israelites in the desert and found some justification for their raising a fuss with Moses for leading them on an apparently fruitless and pointless pilgrimage.

By and by I hauled myself to my feet and continued my journey. A car pulled up and one of the two occupants asked if I were looking for my car. They invited me to get in and we would drive around in search of the elusive vehicle. After some time it remained elusive.

They asked me where I lived. They offered to take me home. I accepted without argument.

I called Fr. C. in Chaska when I thought he would be back from the golf course. He picked me up and we drove to the parking lot where I spotted the car from several blocks away.

I will never forget the Hazeltine U.S. Open -- but I shall certainly try.

My Color Coordinated Canine

by Father Elstan
September 1991

There is, among us columnists of the world, a saying: "When a deadline approaches and no subject presents itself, write about your dog." (Well, if there isn't such a saying, there ought to be.)

But if one is going to present the world's readers of columns the subject of one's canine compassion, one wants to be able to brag about that canine's accomplishments -- He is so smart he can multiply 17 x 84 and get the right answer -- He is so obedient he will swim the Bering Strait to retrieve a polar bear if I ask him to -- He is so brave he will attack a pack of wolves and stay with it till the last one is begging for mercy -- etc.

So when the month rolled around and the time to come up with something approached, I couldn't fall back on Maude for a subject. Her accomplishments were embarrassingly few -- in fact, nonexistent.

Oh, there was a time about four years ago when there was reason to believe she was in a family way. She began to bulge out like she had swallowed a bowling ball, and I presented the fact to the reading public, speaking proudly of the maternal aspect she was assuming, speculating on the number of puppies that might be forthcoming, and, in general, preparing everyone for the happy event. It was a false pregnancy.

I fell back on demonstrating her obedience by giving her negative orders. I would tell folks who showed any interest that she would conform to my every command, and then say, "Maudie, don't roll over," and she didn't. "Maudie, don't shake hands," and she didn't, and so on.

I kept a discreet silence about her intelligence and courage. She was not one of the world's puppy prodigies.

But follow this next bit closely.

About three months ago Chrissy Gregory stopped in and said she would be willing to train Maudie if she could take her for a few hours each week. I said it couldn't be done. She was six years old and in all that time had a clean record. She had never obeyed anybody ever in anything.

Chrissy said, "I can do it."

I said, "Okay, go ahead, but don't expect any results."

As time went on and her education progressed there were signs of results. By the time the county fair came around Chrissy said she was prepared for competition, and would I let her take the little nut to the dog show there. I said, "Sure, go ahead," and prepared myself for yet another frustration.

They came back with a ribbon -- a red one -- but a ribbon, nonetheless. Maude's expert trainer claimed she would have won a blue, but the day of the big contest it was wet and cold outside and Maude showed a certain reluctance to park her rather poorly protected fanny on the cold wet grass. The starry-eyed and critical judges noticed that and deducted a few points, dropping Maude out of the blue ribbon class.

My own version is that Maude realized that blue -- or many other colors -- would clash with her coat, so she took a red. Color coordination means a lot to women.

But next year keep your eyes on the dailies for the headlines and pictures. She's bound to be featured there after the county fair contest.

Gemixte Pickles at the Rectory

by Father Elstan
October 1991

Sue's article in last month's *Gazette*, written in fractured German, triggered my memory.

Father Bernardine and I were stationed together in Chaska in the late '50's. A member of our community, who was the pastor of a nearby church, joined us each evening for prayer, followed by supper. To avoid the use of his real name, shall we refer to him as "Father Sauerkraut"? Why not! He was, for all intents and purposes, kind of a "sauer kraut."

He had come to the U.S. about the time Hitler was starting to kick up his heels. He came complete with the attitude of a Prussian general and the gift of impeccable German. In fact, any incorrect use of his mother tongue was considered by him as tantamount to a sacrilege. If he had read Sue's article I seriously doubt if he would have survived the shock.

Since he felt that way he was, in effect, handing us (Fr. B. and me) what could virtually be considered an embossed invitation to desecrate the German tongue. And we did -- in his presence and with a great display of innocence. Some examples follow:

On one occasion, while we were having supper together, Fr. S.K. was waxing eloquently on the subject of the difficulties he was experiencing in his parish. (Complaining was a favorite pastime of his.) The income was low; the expenses were high; the people were uncooperative; the school kids were disrespectful; and on and on.

In an effort to let him know how we saw it, one of us remarked, "S.K., if the truth were known, 'Du has den Welt bei dem Schwantz over there.' " There was a period of silence as Fr. S.K. struggled with that.

Finally he figured out we were trying to say, "You have the world by the tail over there." Veins stood out on his neck; he grasped his hair and stopped short of rending his garments. Death by apoplexy was just a hair's breadth away.

Fr. S.K. was not above pointing out to us some of his more admirable qualities. We thought the fact that he always showed up promptly for meetings, meals, or whatever, was something that should be commented upon. It took some research to come up with this one . . .

Neither Fr. B. nor I knew what meant "spot" in German, but our old dictionary came to our rescue; and when S.K. showed up that evening -- promptly, as usual -- one of us told him, "S.K., du bist immer Johann auf dem Flecke." ("You are always Johnny-on-the-spot.")

The old veins-in-neck and hair pulling routine kicked in again, mingled with a number of acceptable German phrases. I recall "Dumbkopf" and "Ach du lieber!" and "Schweinhund" being prominent among his responses. Goethe would have been proud of his German eloquence.

Always anxious to say something to build up S.K.'s ego, on an occasion when he made an accurate observation on one of the problems of the day, we remarked, "S.K., du has dem Nagel auf dem Kopf geschlacht." ("You have hit the nail on the head.")

Our compliment didn't meet with the acceptance you might expect. S.K. was within an ace of hurling the furniture, dishes, and other loose articles about the room.

A rich source of English idiom to be translated into literal German came from the field of sports. Father S.K. had made an effort to adopt the interests of his second country and frequently introduced baseball into the conversation. We were always helpful by referring to baseball phrases in high-class Deutsch:

"Die Rot Hosen haben ein duplex-kopfer gespeilt." ("The Red Sox played a double header.")

"Roger Maris hat ein andern heimlauf heute geschlagt." ("Roger Maris hit another home run today.")

"Er hat ein boo-boo in dem aus feld gemacht." ("He made an error in the outfield.")

Fr. S.K.'s veins don't stand out on his neck so much any more. He's gained weight since the '50's. He doesn't tear his hair out anymore. There's none left. Most of it wound up in the vacuum cleaner at the Guardian Angels rectory.

Mostly now, when he sees Fr. B. or me coming, he seeks out a secluded retreat and stays there till we've gone away. He still cringes at the "Gemixte Pickles" we might inflict upon him. The best German he ever heard from us is when we said, "Auf Wiedersehen."

Blessings on Bunions and Dandruff

by Father Elstan
November 1991

Have you ever heard of "The Irish Travelers" -- also referred to as "Irish Gypsies"?

If your life has been spent north of the Mason Dixon line the chances are you've missed them. Their sphere of operation is mostly through the Virginias, the Carolinas, Georgia, and Tennessee.

Their origins seem to go back to the group of nomadic peoples in Ireland who called themselves, "Tinker." It seems they found their way to this country during the potato famine in the Emerald Isle.

Their way of earning their bread and salt is much the same as that used by the gypsy element we know from around here, only the Irish gypsies have elevated their craft to the level of an art form.

Many of them deal in trading automobiles and painting barns and sheds and fences. Once they have painted someone's building for them, they seldom return to that area in their travels. A major ingredient in their paint is water. They work fast, collect fast, and leave the location fast -- before a rainstorm comes along and betrays them and before the local constabulary starts looking into their methods.

When they leave an area it is usually with someone else's pieces of property. They seem to do well financially, judging from the kind of cars and trailers and RVs they drive.

They all subscribe to the Catholic faith, but only to the extent that it doesn't interfere with their life. Mixed up with their Catholicism is a heavy load of superstition.

Once a year a group of them would pull into a park in Memphis, where I was stationed, and as soon as they had settled in, a great many of the women of the group would descend on St. Mary's and spend the entire day in the office -- ordering Masses for the coming year (to be said on specified days, at specified times of the day, for the specified intentions, for stipends that they attempted to specify themselves).

Since they could neither read nor write -- the women Irish gypsies were never allowed to have any schooling; the men completed only the fourth grade level, just enough to be able to read, write, add and subtract -- they had to hang around till they memorized all the specifics of their transactions.

In the course of their annual visits they also ordered dozens of vigil lights, for different times, to be lit by us for them. And they attempted to buy -- or steal

-- every medal, statue, rosary, or anything of a religious nature that they spotted in the office, the waiting room, or on someone's person. It was always a hectic day when the travels of The Irish Travelers brought them to the church.

An even more interesting experience was to visit them in their camp. Anybody coming onto their turf with a Roman collar on or a religious habit was, in essence, inviting a stampede. All the kids, the women, and the men who were sober enough to walk (not a large number) swarmed around demanding that their every ailment from bunions to dandruff be given a blessing -- and every item they had managed to pilfer during their travels across the south land be given the same treatment. It somehow seemed to them to justify the manner in which they had acquired these items.

But they are delightful, different, and interesting people. To their original designation of "Tinker," I would be inclined to add an "s." And may God have mercy on their souls.

The Irish Gypsy Nun

by Father Elstan
December 1991

Pastor Larry Blake dropped by a few weeks ago and in the course of our conversation mentioned that he had found the bit in the *Gazette* last month on the Irish gypsies entirely new to him. He had never heard of them before, which I had suggested in the article was probably the case with most folks who have spent their lives north of the Mason Dixon line.

The article implied that none of the members of that unique group ever escaped from its "different' and rather primitive environment. Few ever did, but there is one notable exception.

One year when a branch of the "tribe" had settled in a public park in Memphis for an extended stay, a swarm of the women of the group swept down on our church (St. Mary's) like the hosts of Midian. Among them was a sixteen-year-old girl named Rosemary Nelson. (Rosemary was not her name. I'm using it because I can't remember her real first name.)

From that time on Rosemary showed up every day -- and in a most inconspicuous manner began to help out everybody that worked out of the church offices and in the church. She helped the secretary in matters that didn't involve reading -- because she couldn't read.

There was a soup kitchen out of the back of the building where she saw the need for volunteers, and she volunteered. There was an outreach program to the elderly poor with offices and a meeting room in the building, and Rosemary saw the need of an extra hand so she put her hand in there.

Occasionally she went into church, knelt down and became absorbed in prayer. In a short time she practically became a fixture around St. Mary's. The staff members remarked how we would miss her when the camp folded up their tents again and silently stole away, and she with them.

But one day when that time was approaching she materialized in my office. Without preamble, and in that peculiar accent of theirs, she said, "Father, I want to stay here when my camp leaves -- and become a Sister."

I was thrilled and frustrated at the same time. The obstacles seemed insurmountable, and I enumerated them. "They will force you to go with them when they leave."

"If I'm not there at the time they will leave wi'out me -- and expect me to catch up later."

"How can you become a Sister? You can't read nor write. You would have to at least be able to do that."

"I'll learn."

"How will you support yourself while you're learning?"

"I'll get a job."

She left me with the distinct impression that none of these things were her problem. They was mine!

Within a few blocks of St. Mary's was St. Joseph Hospital, operated by a group of Franciscan Sisters. I was well acquainted with the "Head Honcho." She was a sister of a classmate of mine. I talked to her about "my" problems. She arranged a job and lodging at the hospital for Rosemary, and one of the Sisters began her education in two of the three "R's" -- reading and writing. But membership in their community was another thing. They had to all be highly degreed and trained nurses.

During her stint with the hospital Sisters, they took her over to the Poor Clare Convent, an order of strict contemplative women. Rosemary was thrilled and decided that was her future.

I left Memphis but was kept informed of her progress. One day I received a letter from her. It was priceless. In bad grammar, bad spelling, and bad punctuation, she outlined her immediate schedule. She was to be received as a member of the Order of St. Clare. Subsequently, she, and a half a dozen others, sent me the account from *The Press Scimitar,* the city of Memphis' paper, plus her and their own accounts.

When the day of her reception came around, all her friends from St. Mary's showed up, her friend from the hospital, the bishop, and a large number of priests -- and her family and most of her old camp. The women were dressed in the finest clothes they could manage to steal for the occasion -- and the men in the discomfort of their sobriety, a concession they made for the event.

Her father led her down the aisle, dignified and sober as an Old Testament patriarch.

She received the name "Sister Mary Anthony." She is serene, peaceful, and happy in her prayerful life as a Poor Clare Sister. It is just possible that she will be the occasion of a transformation in the somewhat offbeat lifestyle of the Irish gypsies of the South.

Roofie Gets Steamed in China

by Father Elstan
January 1992

I'm not quite sure why it is, but Franciscan Orders seems to attract a plethora of people that are best described by the word: "characters." It must be something in the spirit of their founder, St. Francis, that appeals to those who are inclined to ignore society's norms and restrictions.

I was stationed with a prime example of that above in Harbor Springs, Michigan, for several years. His name was Father Rufinus Glauber, hereinafter to be referred to as "Roofie." When he landed in Harbor Springs he was an old man. In the early years of his ministry he was a missionary in China.

The work fit him like a glove. He was way out in the boondocks with poverty-stricken China men, far removed from the niceties and pretentiousness of the more affluent.

He lived in a mud hut with a dirt floor, a beat up old German-made motorcycle, a candle, a table and a cot, and that's about it. From these headquarters he roared around the countryside on his "bike," visiting his far-flung Christian communities, expanding them, and establishing new ones.

He was as happy and free as the chickens and pigs that hung around his quarters and benefited from his proclivity to drop crumbs and other pieces of grub on the floor.

One day a squad of Japanese soldiers showed up at his door. One of the soldiers who could speak a bit of English tried to explain to him that he was under house arrest. Roofie didn't quite catch on. I believe he thought they were protecting his house. He gave them some cigarettes, slapped them on the back, and offered to help them if he could in any way. All in all, it was very cozy.

The next day Roofie flung the door of his house open and roared out on his bike -- and waved at his "protectors" as he disappeared down a path through a rice field, shouting to them not to wait up for him. He would be gone for three days. The Japanese said, "Hi!" and "Ah So!" and a number of other things, as they displayed a lot of agitated consternation.

Three days later Roofie came back, as he had predicted, passed out cigarettes to the soldiers, slapped them on the back, and thanked them warmly for their fraternal concern.

The next day an officer of the Japanese Imperial Army was waiting outside the door of Roofie's abode and stopped the bike before Roofie could get up a head of steam. He was a man of stern views and visage, and he took a dim view of the easygoing relationship between his men and our friend, and in no uncertain terms made it clear that he, Roofie, could not travel around in this uninhibited manner. From now on he was to go no farther than 14 ½ paces from his front door.

Roofie objected that he was an American citizen and he could go anywhere he wanted to any time he chose. Of all the wrong things he might have said, reminding a Japanese at that time in history that he was an American citizen was possibly the worst. The man was unimpressed.

He started to shove Roofie back into his hut, whereupon Roofie decked him. Immediately he, Roofie, was surrounded by half a dozen soldiers with bayonets pressed up against his rather impressive stomach. He went into his house and brooded for the next three weeks, unable to grasp why he was such a threat to the designs of the Japanese Empire.

Finally, through the efforts of some big wheels in the Vatican, most of our missionaries in China were repatriated, Roofie included. But he never wasted a chance to belabor our superior to send him back to China, which, of course, was impossible then, and is to the present day.

Roofie Raids the Refrigerator

by Father Elstan
February 1992

You may have met "Roofie" (Father Rufinus) in this column last month. You will recall he was missionary in China at the time the Japanese marched into that country and more or less effectively put a lid on Christian proselytizing. As a result, Roofie was confined to his house where he sat and simmered until some deft work in high places sprung him and he was repatriated.

Back in the U.S. he stormed around through the Midwest, helping where he was needed, and preaching wherever he was invited -- chiefly on the subject of missions.

Roofie's mode of transportation was whatever was most available at the time. If that happened to be a car, that wasn't available to him for very long, as he had a habit of hitting solid objects, stripping the gears, and generally rendering the machine inoperable.

He used public transportation a lot, but often wound up elsewhere from where he intended to go. He wasn't above walking and hitchhiking, and whenever he arrived at his destination, usually late, he always had a gripping story to tell of his adventure.

And when he arrived he was usually hungry. Since he was schooled in the Chinese missions, the kind of food was of no great concern to him. As long as he could chew it and swallow it he did so with great zest and proclaimed it the best he'd ever eaten -- no matter what it was.

On one memorable occasion he was scheduled to help out a priest in some remote village in the boot heel area of Missouri. The pastor told him where to find the house key, in case he came in late and the place was locked up for the night. True to form, Roofie came in late and, also true to form, hungry.

He made a beeline for the refrigerator. There sat an open can of some kind of meat spread which he smeared on several pieces of bread. As he ate contentedly he was approached by the pastor's dog, a huge but gentle mastiff. Gentle though he was, he seemed to take a dim view of Roofie's making himself at home like that and growled occasionally to let it be known that he disapproved. Roofie placated the beast with an occasional bit of his supper.

The next morning the pastor, the dog, and Roofie gathered in the kitchen for breakfast. The pastor opened the refrigerator and said, "Hey, I wonder what happened to that can of dog food I had in here for King Saul!"

Roofie Lands With a Thud

by Father Elstan
March 1992

We find ourselves following the fortunes of "Roofie" (Father Rufinus) as he bounced his way through life. He had been run out of China by the soldiers of the honorable Empire of the Rising Sun; he held different jobs in his native country after his return; and he finally landed -- with a thud -- in Harbor Springs, Michigan, where I was stationed at the time.

Various friars, who have been stationed with him, asked if we had sturdy doors on our house. I opined that they were reasonably sturdy, and the inevitable response was: "They had better be more than that."

Another question was: "How strong is your furniture?" Answer: "It's Viking Oak. It's supposed to last the life of the building." Response: "Wanna bet?" I was apprehensive.

Roofie roared in shortly after these exchanges like a typhoon out of the China Sea. With a broad gesture he knocked over a rather nice end table with a lamp on it. He didn't seem to notice.

As I was picking up the pieces he landed in a chair like he had just plunged through the roof and managed, by a stroke of great good fortune, to hit the right spot. The chair held up, but barely.

After a few minutes of conversation I showed him to his room. He walked in and slammed the door, loosening some plaster on the ceiling which, with subsequent slams, fell to the floor.

I always thought it was providential that Roofie had been in the Chinese missions. His appearance was that of a huge animated Buddha statue. He must have made a great impression on his oriental flock, resembling, as he did, their favorite god.

As time went on he developed an arthritic condition that bowed his legs out to point where he looked like a Buddha statue perched on two sturdy limbs put together to form a complete circle. It often occurred to me that if his legs were straightened out he would be twelve feet tall.

Roofie was at his most typical when he made himself breakfast. After his Mass in the morning he waddled into the kitchenette, which was an adjunct to the living room. His breakfast was simple: two pieces of toast with butter and jam and a glass of orange juice.

By the time he got done spreading the butter and jam, some of which actually got on the toast, and pouring the orange juice, some of which hit the glass, the kitchen looked like an earthquake scene that had been hit by a tornado.

Always conscious of cleanliness, when he was finished eating, Roofie would take the end of his sleeve and sweep it over the table top and dispose of the residue onto the floor -- "Just like we did in China. The chickens and pigs would always clean it up." He failed to notice we didn't house chickens and pigs in our quarters.

The broken glass and dropped silverware stayed where they landed. The refrigerator door usually stayed open. The pictures that had been knocked sideways remained sideways.

After this routine, Roofie huffed and puffed his way to a chair and plopped down with evident relief where he said some prayers and rested his aching knees and legs. During his calm time the furniture got a reprieve, the plaster hung on, and the doors rested calmly on their hinges.

Roofie the Cornball Character

by Father Elstan
April 1992

To further embellish the picture of the person who was "Roofie," Friar Rufinus, I should mention that by the time he barged into Harbor Springs he was blind in one eye, beleaguered by arthritic knees, and rounded out to such an extent he presented the perfect picture of Shakespeare's classic Friar Tuck.

He was the "all American volunteer." Anything that had to be done, he was ready and willing to step in and do it whether his physical deficiencies were a hindrance or not.

He volunteered to take on several religion classes in the school. The kids would have to come over to the house and help him across the yard and up to the classroom where he would crash into a seat and carry on with his life's experiences -- mostly drawn from his time in the Chinese missions.

It took the entire class to get him over there and back, and the entire class was always most anxious to be of assistance. This solemn procession took place several times every week.

Roofie always wanted to take a public Mass whenever possible. There, too, he drew upon his colorful past for stories to illustrate a point. After about a year and a half he ran out of stories and so started all over again, applying them to different lessons, however tenuous the connection between the story and the point.

His saying a Mass was always an adventure. Because of the fact that he couldn't see out of one eye, and was congenitally clumsy to start with, and had a remarkable disregard for details, he generally went out to the altar with his vestments askew and, not infrequently, on backwards.

Once at the altar he frequently managed to upset the cruets, knock over a candle, or drop the book on the floor. The servers at his Mass always had extra duties to perform, which they did with shy smiles, apparently unobserved by Roofie.

Roofie enjoyed telling jokes, which he did over and over again -- the same ones. His shortcoming in this department was always that he couldn't distinguish between which jokes were cornball and which were not. I got into the habit of paying little attention to his jokes, giving them merely a token smile when he finished telling them.

But one day he crossed me up. I had two toy dachshunds in the house whom I was trying to teach the ways of polite society. One day, after observing my efforts, he said, "That reminds me," and went on to tell about the guy who was trying to train his dog. Each time the dog "misbehaved," the man would rub the culprit's nose in it and then take him and throw him out the window. After about two weeks of this routine the man thought he had finally gotten through. He saw the dog rub his nose in the proper place -- but then he ran over and jumped out the window.

I gave his story my usual unenthusiastic smile -- and let it go at that, until suddenly it dawned on me that it was funny. Roofie told the story five more times in the next two weeks.

Haven't You Heard?

by Father Elstan
May 1992

We've pretty well exhausted the subject of "Roofie" and his uniqueness. He was introduced as an example of the several of our friars who can best be categorized as "characters."

Another is a man who has been in pastoral work his entire life. In that capacity he has encountered every kind of being that graces the human scene -- as anyone whose work is similar can testify is standard experience.

Each parish seems to be blessed with at least one member, depending on the size of the parish, whose vocation in life is to write anonymous letters to the pastor. It is well that they do so since, generally, they, the authors, need the practice in spelling, composition, punctuation, and journalistic accuracy. What they are usually accomplished in, and need no practice in, is in being venomously critical.

Father X received just such a letter on one occasion. It was unusually juvenile in language, syntax, and spelling, even by standards of anonymous letter writers, so much so that it was humorous in the extreme. Father X, in a kindly attempt to respond, published the letter in totality in the parish bulletin. Virtually everybody in the parish, with the exception of one, was laughing heartily for the next few weeks.

Father X had a few more tricks up his sleeve. Some communities seem to be fertile breeding grounds for outlandish rumors. He was the pastor in just such a place. Many of the rumors originated with the members of his choir. He decided to start his own rumor ...

One day, when the choir was practicing, he wandered into the choir loft and when there was a break in the music and conversation, he said, "Is there anything to the rumor that the Pope is going to stop here at our church in two weeks?" In the ensuing hubbub he drifted away.

Three days later the choir was back practicing music appropriate for a papal visit. Father X walked back up to the choir loft and asked what this extra practice and unusual music was all about.

"Haven't you heard, Father? The Pope is going to be here at 2:30 p.m. on the 14th."

On another occasion, when it would have the most effect, he remarked. "I heard (or maybe, "They say ...") that the bishop is going to forbid anybody living within a mile of our cemetery to be buried there."

A few days later a delegation, properly dressed and looking serious and official, stopped at the church and asked to see the pastor. The spokesman for the group explained they thought it was proper for him to know they were going to confront the bishop about his new ruling.

"Several of us live within a mile of the cemetery, and we want to be buried there."

Father X pointed out to them that they couldn't be buried any place while they were still living. They would have to die first.

Father X had some outlandish rumor going there almost constantly. The more unbelievable it was, the more it was swallowed.

PRINTS OF A PRIEST

Fr. Pat and the "Krick"

by Father Elstan
June 1992

It is now time for you to meet Father Pat O'Brien. He was just far enough ahead of me in the seminary that I didn't meet him until after I was ordained. But the stories about him from those who were acquainted with his wit and wisdom made me feel like I knew him before I met him.

He was from Ashland, Wisconsin, an iron ore shipping port city on Lake Superior. His brothers and sisters were numerous. The family's income was limited. Neither of these factors seemed to have an adverse effect on Pat's psyche. It did, though, give him a healthy disdain for material things and an almost total absence of dependence on them.

A suggestion of the origin of his wit and wisdom comes from a story he loved to tell about his grandfather. His grandfather rose in city politics, in the course of his illustrious career, to the exalted position of city councilman in the city of Ashland (pop. 10,000).

Through the center of this mighty metropolis there flowed a creek (or "krick," as he, Pat, pronounced it). The location of the "krick" made passage from one side of town to the other somewhat difficult, and there gradually developed a movement among the citizens of the city to get the administration to build a bridge over it.

Argument arose; sides were taken; families became divided; some decision had to be made. Father Pat's grandfather -- frugal with own money (by necessity) and with other people's, the taxpayers' (on principle) -- was anti-bridge. The city council met to hammer out a conclusion to the problem that was dividing their fair city.

The pro-bridge faction presented their arguments, well-worded and well-thought out. The anti-bridge group did the same. There seemed to be a deadlock. Tempers were flaring. Arguments were becoming personal.

Finally, Pat's granddad arose to address the city fathers. He concluded his presentation with the statement, "That krick is so small I can go to the bathroom halfway across it." (The exact wording of his final argument may have become distorted in the course of time. For those interested in historical accuracy they may consult the minutes of the meeting of the Ashland City Council, dated April 3rd, 1886.)

The president of the city council was shocked and offended. He rose to say so as he pounded his gavel to restore order. He drew himself up to his full height and in a voice befitting his exalted position said, "Mr. O'Brien, you're out of order!" To which Mr. O'Brien retorted, "Of course I am. If I weren't, I'd be able to go to the bathroom all the way across that krick!" (Again, for the exact wording refer to the minutes of the meeting of the Ashland City Council, dated April 3rd, 1886.)

The question of the bridge was not settled that night, and I'm not sure how it was subsequently settled, but I thought this incident from the family history of Fr. Pat might give you some understanding of events in his life that we will record subsequently.

Fr. Pat and His Upholstery

by Father Elstan
July 1992

In last month's installment we attempted to present a distant look at Father Pat O'Brien's person by stealing a page from modern sociology which tends to search our ancestry for an excuse for our deficiencies and faults.

In his case, however, we went back to his grandfather to find a explanation for his quick wit and engaging humor.

I never met any of his ancestors, so I'm not sure which one or ones were responsible for his being stocky and muscular, and bearing a complexion that strongly resembled an inflamed liver. Decorating that complexion of his face was a heavy black growth of whiskers that make their presence known after about 10:30 a.m. each day, regardless of how zealously he applied his razor in the earlier hours of the morning.

Crowning all of this was a head of hair which, in the earlier years of his existence, presented the picture of a head of hair that was innocent of the caress of a comb. In later years the need for a comb diminished dramatically, but there always remained just enough whispers of the stuff to give our hero a disheveled look.

A first glance at that picture would suggest that Pat's voice, if it were to be consistent with the rest of his description, would have the quality of a pirate captain's dishing it out to his crew. In reality, his voice came closer to that of a slightly agitated mouse. The adjective most frequently used by someone making reference to the tone and timber of Pat's voice was "squeaky."

In matters of attire Pat's choice was determined by what was most convenient and closest at hand. The idea of color coordination had completely escaped him. And the presence of loose threads and holes and foreign matter on a garment never deterred him from wearing it.

And even on those rare occasions when he had to be a bit more circumspect with regard to his upholstery and don his best pair of black pants and clerical shirt -- a meeting, perhaps, where the bishop would be present, or other dignitaries -- within five minutes of his struggling into these freshly cleaned and pressed items he would present a strong resemblance to a sack of cats.

The press in the pants would disappear; a shirt button would pop off; his belt would be off center; and bags would appear at the knees. How Pat could bring about this unusual effect remains one of the great unsolved mysteries of our time.

Divine Providence was undoubtedly doing its job well when Pat was ordained and sent to Our Lady, Help of Christians Parish in Bastrop, Louisiana. One could search far and wide to find a flock where material things were more conspicuously absent -- or where, for that matter, a clergyman clothed haphazardly and shaven less cleanly would cause fewer remarks behind the hand.

And Pat blended in like he was meant for the job. He went about his work with his people with zest and zeal and in high good humor.

You may wish to keep these paragraphs handy as a reference when we present examples of my frequent contact with Pat over a span of years that came to an end with his sudden death in May of 1975 or 1976. I don't recall exactly. What I do recall is that it was a sad day for the many people in high and low places who loved him dearly.

Fr. Pat's Basketball and Bean Soup

by Father Elstan
August 1992

So let's get on with outlining Friar Patrick O'Brien, whom we introduced to you in the last two of these columns.

There was more to him than a square jaw perpetually sporting stubbly undergrowth, a voice in the higher octave, and an aura that was obviously Irish. Among other gifts he had an uncanny ability to quote the classics and Holy Writ in a telling way, but in contexts not originally intended by the author.

When he was assigned to the Church of Our Lady, Help of Christians, one of his confreres dropped him off on the parish grounds. Pat looked out at the scene and proclaimed it: "The abomination of desolation spoken of by the prophet Jeremiah." He wasn't far from wrong.

His church consisted of two old army barracks donated (I think) by a local military base -- probably Shreveport -- and hauled in and deposited on the parish grounds. The two buildings were held together by some tar paper, a few stray boards, and the blessing of the previous pastor.

Alongside the school, the church looked rather classy. There were twelve grades, all under one roof -- if you could call it a roof. The air conditioning consisted of broken windows and missing boards and whatever breezes happened along.

Pat and eight or ten Sisters taught all the classes, Pat teaching subjects in high school that he had never taken himself. But he got results.

Pat's athletic program consisted almost exclusively of basketball. Every senior boy was on the team, most of the juniors and a sprinkling of sophs and freshmen. And they practiced every recess, and after school until the sun went down -- except when the moon was full -- with Pat giving them encouragement, strategy, moves, and plays. In the summertime they practiced all day.

If the church was dilapidated and the school primitive, the basketball court was prehistoric. The backboard consisted of a few broken boards attached to a pole that stood at an angle. The basket was a bent rim that also hung at an angle, attached by a couple of bent and loose bolts.

The rim, as Pat put it, was "sans webbing." The court upon which Pat prepared his charges was either dusty or muddy -- but always uneven. That may explain why Pat and his lads consistently won the state tournament in their class and frequently beat up on schools ten times bigger in number and always bigger in stature.

When his kids got on a court that was hard and level -- and when they could shoot at a flat backboard that held steady when the ball hit it -- and shot for a rim that was sturdy and solid, they were in hog heaven; and the game was a breeze for them after the conditions under which they had practiced.

Pat also attributed his success to another factor as well. Before each game -- which was never a home game, nobody else would play on Pat's court -- Pat always fed his troops a huge meal of baked beans and hot dogs. He claimed it gave them that extra something in terms of vitality and staying power. It also gave them occasion for some rather low high school humor.

They traveled to the games in a bus, driven by Pat, that matched the general decor of the place. It traveled more on flat tires than on full ones. The doors were more often leaning against the garage than containing its passengers; and the engine, when it worked at all, did so reluctantly.

But they always made it there and back, rarely, however, on schedule; but they didn't want to go too fast anyway because the brakes seldom worked.

The team's uniforms were a sight to behold. There were never any two that matched but they could always be identified as the uniforms of Our Lady, Help of Christians (referred to by the parishioners as "Our Lady, H'ep of Christians").

Their logo was, of course, OLHC, and sometimes the letters were in the wrong order, and usually one or two letters were missing on their jerseys. School officials in Louisiana viewed OLHC with disbelief and dismay. Some even wrote long dissertations, explaining Father Pat's academic and athletic success with his charges, seldom ascribing it to dedication, devotion, hard work -- or bean soup.

Very few of his students dropped out of school and most of the team went on to college. Many of them made the college team. Not a few of them wound up in the NBA. The corporate minds of the education system in Louisiana applied its massive might to explaining away Pat's success and always came up confused.

The explanation was simple. That was Pat.

Fr. Pat and His Sacred Clubs

by Father Elstan
September 1992

More on Father Pat O'Brien. From past installments you may have gotten the impression his sphere of action was in a neighborhood where the word "affluence" didn't apply. If so, your impression was accurate. He recalled with some glee how, the first Sunday he was there, after the last Mass was over, he put the entire collection in his shirt pocket and went up to the monastery where he ate and slept and kept his records.

He dumped his "take" out on the table and counted it, and dutifully entered it into his ledger -- $1.37. He liked to refer to his parish as a model of unity in the church: "One Faith, One Baptism, and One Dollar in the Sunday Collection."

If your impression from past installments was that Pat's parish was poor (and your impression was accurate), you may also have concluded from these installments that his interest in sports centered solely around basketball. That conclusion needs correcting.

In his younger years he slung a mean curve ball and embarrassed many a batter. In later years he developed a keen interest in golf. But his equipment was reduced to the least common denominator. I doubt if he ever hit a brand new ball in his life, nor one that wasn't scarred or lopsided.

The tees he used were cracked and usually missing the bottom half. His club set consisted of a driver -- with the tape on the shaft dangling loose and the club head caked with Louisiana mud -- from which protruded pieces of grass and twigs, a sand wedge, a 3-wood, and a putter. From any distance after his drive he would use the 3-wood and, as he put it, "finesse it onto the green."

Pat had a reverence for his clubs that didn't go to the extent of cleaning them up. Perhaps he thought that if he removed the mud and grass from them, they would be thrown off balance.

On one occasion he was heading out on a vacation. No vacation was complete for him that didn't include golf. He tied his four clubs together with a piece of frayed binder twine and brought them into the airport with his battered suitcase. The man checking the baggage through looked at Pat's luggage and sports equipment with a mixture of amazement and disbelief. Then he picked up the clubs and, handling them as if they were contaminated with agent orange, threw them as far as he could upon the conveyor belt.

Pat noticed the rough handling of his sacred clubs and disapproved. He gave voice: "Hey, those are my golf clubs! (I guess it was well that he identified the items. The man was probably wondering what they were.) If they aren't delivered at their destination in good condition I will hold the airline responsible!" (I can hear the man saying under his breath, "Well, they didn't arrive here in very good condition.")

At the monastery Pat commandeered two rooms, one for his bedroom and another -- with a bed in it for a guest -- which he used as a storeroom. In the latter he stored books, clothes, sporting equipment, odd pieces of machinery that had fallen off his bus and car and lawnmower, and sundry other items.

On one occasion a guest stopped by and was to stay overnight. Pat led him to the guest room. When he opened the door he said, "I can't put you in here. This room is kind of dirty. I'll sleep in here. You take my room."

The guest's reaction was similar to that of the baggage man at the airport. Pat told him, "When you get unpacked come on down to the kitchen. I'll fix you supper. "Supper" was a can of sardines and a box of saltine crackers.

Well, that was Pat!

Fr. Pat, the "Clazy Amelican"

by Father Elstan
October 1992

Let's have one last visit with Father Pat O'Brien, shall we?

One facet of his fascinating character was his ability to communicate. It's no wonder he communicated something, since he generally kept up a steady stream of chatter whenever anyone was within hearing distance.

A couple of examples of Pat's communication skills showed up when five of us, on the occasion of our silver jubilee, took an around-the-world tour. Pat was three years late with his celebration, but he felt justified in taking advantage of the offer -- "retroactively," as he put it.

We were in Rome, at the bottom of the Victor Emmanual monument. There are three hundred and some steps to the top of this colossus. Tourists who are still in prime condition struggle to the top to view the seven hills of Rome and the roof tops of virtually the entire city. These attractions, when balanced against the necessary exertion to see them, lost their fascination for Pat. He opted to stay at the bottom and wait for the rest of us.

When we came back down, Pat was in animated conversation with three of Rome's finest. He and they were laughing hilariously and gesticulating vigorously. When we asked him what it was all about, he said he had gotten directions to the closest "biffy."

Now Pat didn't know any Italian, and they didn't know any English; and we were reasonably sure that whatever quotations he may have used from Cicero, Ovid, or Pliny didn't suffice to do the trick. He had to accomplish his communication by gestures, so we had to conclude that the only reason he escaped being hauled into court was the lax standards of the Italian constabulary.

Later on in the trip we landed in Hong Kong. To get from hither to yon one day, we boarded a public transportation vehicle. The machine was packed with hoards of neatly uniformed, black-haired, slant-eyed, grade school kids. Within minutes they were babbling Chinese to Pat, giggling uncontrollably, and reciting their lessons to him.

Pat jabbered on in English -- and they seemed to understand each other. It was one of the most extraordinary communication events I've ever witnessed. And I've often wondered if there are some twenty-six to thirty-year-old Chinese in Hong Kong today who still remember that "Clazy Amelican" to whom they recited their lessons on a streetcar on Lotus Blossom Street some twenty years ago. But that was Pat.

Getting Steamed on Mondays

by Father Elstan
November 1992

I'm in a bad state of mind. I could almost say I'm steamed.

To start with, it's a Monday. Western civilization -- nor Eastern, for that matter -- has never, with all its technological advances, managed to circumvent Monday on the calendar.

But it's not just Monday. It's one of those Mondays when I pay bills that have accumulated with alarming rapidity, and in a very short period of time. If there is one thing besides the astounding amounts of these bills, it's the manner in which they are presented that shoot the old pressure up to record highs and cause the sweat glands to function at full force.

Here's one for $3.27. It comes with three large sheets of paper -- all identical -- tightly typewritten in code, except for the necessary directive: "Pay upon receipt." (I hardly intended to pay the bill before I got it.) I know it's for $3.27 -- that's the last in a long series of figures. I know what the bill is for, also. It's for Item #3725869.

Here's one that insists on me writing the account number on the check. I always wondered why. They have the bill enclosed. They have the check. One time in a high dudgeon I sent the check off without the account number written on the check as they had directed -- just to see what would happen. Nothing did.

Here's one that directs me to use the correct postage on the envelope. If they hadn't told me to do that, I certainly wouldn't have. Once, in a spirit of defiance, I put an extra stamp on the envelope -- one of those ridiculous ones from the post office issued when the price went from 25 cents to 29 cents. Remember them? "This U.S. stamp, along with 25 cents of additional U.S. postage, is equivalent to the 'F' stamp rate." I waited in vain to hear from this creditor. Nothing was ever forthcoming.

And aren't those phone bills enough to tie your knots? There are never any long distance calls on the phone in the Parish Center, but it takes the phone company many man-hours and nine pages of figures to arrive at $0.00 at the bottom of the bill.

Here's one that gives invaluable advice: "Please disregard this bill if you have already paid it." Please!

This one has probably prevented thousands of customers from placing the bill in the envelope correctly: "Be sure our address shows in the window of the return envelope" -- "before mailing." Now, really!

Here's the gas bill. That's always good for a laugh with its wealth of unintelligible information: BTU multiplier; Pressure multiplier; Gas used in 29 days; 148 CCF; Com/Ind firm rate; Customer charge (includes 3 CCF); Gas charge (145 CCF @ $.41800); Interim rate adjustment (63.61 x 2.6300%); Purchased gas adjustment (148 CCF @ $.05770 - $8.45).

Total current billing is $73.82 -- but the amount due is twice that much! No wonder at the end of a Monday like this I have disheveled hair, a wild stare, and a curt manner when the phone rings.

The prize is the bill that prints on the outside of the envelope detailed instructions on how to open it. Following these instructions to the letter invariably results in a broken fingernail, a paper cut on the thumb, and the contents of the envelope torn into shreds by the time they are removed. That's what *used* to happen. I now open these missives with a letter opener, as I do with all the others, thus saving myself endless aggravation.

Ah, this one makes sense. It's almost a pleasure to pay it, except for the fact that it's a four-figure item. It simply says: "Please remit." But even here they could have left off the "Please remit" part. I am fully aware that a bill is meant to be remitted.

Oh well, to summarize it all in the parlance of the gas bill: "T.G.N.M.M.F.A.W." Thank God, No More Monday For Another Week.

If Maude Had Visited Bethlehem

by Father Elstan
December 1992

I picture Maude, my toy dachshund, present at the events surrounding the most significant occurrence in the history of the universe -- the birth of Christ.

If she had been in residence at the motel where Mary and Joseph wanted to stop for the night, she would have missed the majesty of those two and probably barked at them -- not unlike the man who turned them out.

As they looked for a place to stay she may well have traipsed after them, winding up in the cave where they settled down. Her first order of business would be to establish a working relationship with the other animals present, talking things over with the mule, hassling the goat, and curling up close to the cow for warmth -- not unlike her human counterparts who allow relationships of secondary importance to supplant the truly important one, Christ.

Maude wakes up in the morning to find a new member in their community. She checks him out. He's an object of curiosity and an occasion for an emotional binge -- as any baby is. Like so many of her human "superiors," she misses the point. In her case, of course, it's not her fault. There is no malice.

Her sleep is disturbed in the middle of the night by a group of men driving sheep ahead of them. This is intolerable, waking someone up in the middle of the night with a sheep roundup. But the noise is replaced with music, such as she has never before heard; and like her human counterparts, she fails to identify the music of heaven.

After a few days -- during which time Maude learns how to get Mary's attention; how to con food out of Joseph; how to get the most comfortable spot in the stable; in general, how to use the event of Christ's birth for her own purposes, not unlike some of her human counterparts -- more visitors show up. These visitors carry strange odors with them, besides the ones emanating from the strange animals they are riding. She sniffs out the incense and the myrrh as if they are her personal property and gives her unqualified approval. Because of the delight these new scents provided her, she probably identifies Christmas with fascinating smells. Well, that's not as far off as some of her human counterparts who equate Christmas with chestnuts roasting on an open fire.

In fact, between now and December 25th, we will be told by many experts what Christmas is *all* about, of what it means: "Sleigh bells in the snow." When's the last time you heard sleigh bells in the snow or any place else?

Christmas means "giving." Christmas means "getting." Christmas means "children." Christmas means "shopping." Christmas means "carols." Christmas means some ruminant that looks like he got his nose in the home brew. Like Maude, we are going to too easily identify Christmas with corollaries, its adjuncts, or elements that are totally irrelevant.

Christmas is God becoming man, and in doing so entered the human condition. He involved a human mother. He became dependent on a human protector and provider. He dealt with the world of commerce (the hotel manager). He was born in the home of animals. He mixed with the poor (the shepherds) and the wealthy (the kings from the Orient). A star that He created was an item there. Maude missed all that and sometimes so do we.

The Monsignor's Arrogant Cat

by Father Elstan
January 1993

The rectory this tale comes from was one in Chicago back a few years. The story still circulates around the archdiocese.

The personnel involved in this gripping tale of intrigue are, first of all, the Monsignor who guided the spiritual destinies of a large parish and presided over events within the walls of the priests' house. Also within those walls was a typical priest's housekeeper, whose overriding aim in life was to keep her three men overfed. The two other men were assistants to the Msgr.

The fourth celebrity in this drama was the Msgr.'s cat. According to the Msgr., nothing was too good for this favored feline. All considerations took into account the well-being and comfort of the cat in preference to the convenience of the two assistants and the housekeeper.

An obvious example of this prevailing attitude was what occurred at the evening meal each day. There was a stool alongside the Msgr.'s chair and a small silver bell at the Msgr.'s place. When all was ready, the Msgr. rang the bell and, shortly, the supercilious cat strode into the dining room, snubbed the two assistants and the housekeeper, hopped upon his place of honor beside the Msgr., and waited to be served.

Without waiting for the completion of the grace before meals, he inhaled what he was served and then crept off to a comfortable corner, followed by the Msgr.'s indulgent smile, to digest what he had inhaled, and contemplated the benefits of his privileged status.

The constant repetition of this scene became intolerable to the victims of it. Dark plots were forged to eliminate the cat. Even murder was given some thought -- of the cat, of course -- but every scheme seemed to have a flaw, something that might be detected by the Msgr.

The time came for the Msgr.'s annual vacation. Plotting progressed more freely. Divine inspiration struck one of the assistants. He outlined his dark intrigue to his other two accomplices in wine, and his plan was adopted unanimously.

Suppertime came, and the cat's bell was rung, signaling the beginning of the meal. As was the custom, the cat strode in and took his place, after giving the three lesser members of the household an arrogant sneer.

Next to the assistant closest to the cat was the holy water sprinkler. When the cat was thoroughly engrossed in his favorite activity, the assistant picked up the sprinkler, showed it to the cat, and then, with good wrist action and a fine follow-through, belted the aristocratic head of the cat between the ears. Supper was forgotten. Our hero screeched and then streaked off to a remote part of the premises -- to contemplate his mortality and the injustices of life.

This process was repeated periodically over the few weeks until the return of the Msgr., who could hardly wait till supper time for his happy reunion with the only being in his life that counted.

When they were being seated, one of the two plotters told the Msgr. that in his absence a peculiar circumstance had arisen. The cat had become possessed by the devil. Whenever he came into close proximity to holy water, he screeched and ran and acted like he was in agonizing torture. To convince the Msgr., they procured the holy water sprinkler and invited the Msgr. to ring the bell. He did. The cat responded. He was shown the instrument of his misery and reacted as predicted.

The Msgr. was convinced. Immediately after the meal he gathered up the afflicted cat and hauled him into the inner city where he was released to seek his fortune in the alleys and garbage cans of the hostile metropolis. His happy years were, from that point on, limited in number and intensity.

May your new year be limited in happiness in no way.

The Gravel Pit King

by Father Elstan
February 1993

In 1967 I was sent to Harbor Springs, Michigan. Within five minutes of arriving there, it was abundantly evident that the most pressing need at the place was a new monastery.

The old one was built some time during the IIIrd Olympiad. It was three stories high, all frame, built to house thirteen friars, but was presently housing two. In addition to the two friars, however, it was home to several large families of mice -- and squirrels were regular callers, and some other regular residents.

The wiring, I believe, had been done by Thomas Edison. Each room had a woodburning stove which hadn't been lighted for a long time for obvious reasons. It was a moot question whether the place would fall down before it burnt down. I hoped to tear it down before either of the above happened.

There was a prominent lawyer in the parish whose judgment I respected, and I presented him with our problem. He endorsed the concept of a new home for the friars enthusiastically -- and volunteered to organize the resort people of the parish into a fundraising group. (He felt he could expect a response from them if he asked because over the years of time he had rescued many of their progeny from the clutches of the law by means of his legal expertise.)

Within a week he had them -- about twenty -- and me committed to a golf game nearby. After the game there was a sumptuous lunch, and the project was outlined for all present. The response was positive for all around, but no one mentioned any specific sums.

I walked out of the dining room of the club house with a wrinkled brow and dull eye, which were occasioned by my misgivings.

But out in the parking lot, one of those who had been present came up to me, placed his hand on my shoulder, and told me not to worry. Whatever amount was still lacking after all the results were in would surely be forthcoming. Our new home will be built and paid for in full; I could rest assured.

I was heartened. I was even more heartened when I found out this gentleman had a monopoly on the gravel pits in the state of Illinois.

A few weeks later this generous soul invited me to dinner at his summer home. I went with a healthy appetite and prepared to ask for a Southern Comfort Manhattan on the rocks when offered a drink before dinner. I anticipated, too, coming home with a substantial check in the old wallet.

No drink was forthcoming. The meal might just as well not have come forth; mine host was a vegetarian of the strongest views. All this celebration took place in the most Spartan of settings, under the eye of a stern and sullen looking man-servant. After the revelries were complete, I went home -- without a check. But I expected it to materialize in the future.

The building went up. The funds to pay for it came in in sufficient quantities to cover the expenses -- and then some. I virtually forgot about the gravel pit king, until one day a huge brown envelope came by registered mail from him. I confess to some shaking of the hand as I opened it.

Two impressive looking documents fell out. One was a stock certificate for a company in New York worth $1.45. But the other was a piece of stock in some branch of Sears and Roebuck that was long since defunct. The total worth of this stock was $2.04.

I immediately invested the grand total in blue chip stock, and it is reaping huge dividends for the parish to this day.

The Burden of Headgear

by Father Elstan
March 1993

Let's look into my lifelong relationship with hats.

When we were growing up on our 120 acres in Scott County, every summer vacation started with my brother and me going into Sander's General Store in Jordan and investing 25 cents in a straw hat. It was almost a ritual.

For perhaps two days the hats looked grand, but before long they became battered, spattered, and burdened with fishing equipment hanging from the brim. We liked it that way, since it added to our Huckleberry Finn image along with our bare feet and overalls (pronounced "overhauls") held up by one suspender.

Then I joined the Franciscan Order and was issued a brown habit that featured a cowl which served as a handy luggage carrier when in the "off" position. Usually the luggage it carried was a Ping Pong ball or piece of fruit clandestinely deposited there by one of my too exuberant confreres. When the weather was cold the cowl flipped up very handily.

For civilian wear, called "civvies," we had to have a black hat. I rarely wore it, mainly because I was constantly losing it, and I never felt comfortable in it. When I was in St. Paul, Bishop Brady noticed that many of his priests were coming to meetings and celebrations sans black hat, and issued an executive order to correct the abuse. I went downtown and bought a black hat. The next day I was transferred to Memphis where I was happy to hear no such burden was placed upon us.

For the next many years I simply wore, when necessary, whatever headgear was available -- usually something left behind by a previous member of the community. And so I arrived in Victoria, where I came across a hat that was meant for the climate. It was large and fuzzy, came down over the ears, and when worn gave its wearer the appearance of one who had just walked out of the Gulag archipelago.

I didn't concern myself with appearances but was more aware of the utilitarian aspect of the hat. But I couldn't help notice subdued snickers and surreptitiously pointed fingers when I appeared in public wearing my warm hat. Some were even emboldened to make smart aleck remarks about my appearance within range of my hearing. I decided to consider the source of these remarks, concentrate on the practical aspects of my headgear, and bear the humiliations that accompanied it with saintly stoicism.

Then one day a box, beautifully wrapped and topped off with a red bow, appeared on the sacristy table. There was no note or name on the box, and I assumed it was something left over from a Valentine's Day children's liturgy where the kids brought gifts of various descriptions to the altar at the offertory procession.

I was carrying the box to the wastebasket when I noticed something inside slide back and forth. I opened the box -- and there was a hat, a classic derby with ear flaps, a chapeau that the most distinguished in the land could wear for any occasion without apologies to anyone.

To my benefactor -- if he or she is reading this column -- I wish to express my undying gratitude for silencing the sneers, snickers, and snide remarks of the public, and for providing me with a head cover that is at the same time sharp and practical.

I Have a Dream

by Father Elstan
April 1993

So it's March, and you'd jolly well better be interested in basketball or you're pretty much out of it.

Try to get the news and the weather prediction, and the odds are when the picture comes on your TV screen, you will see some seven-foot giant dangling from the rim of a basket after having tried to demolish the backboard, the basket, and the frame sustaining the two. Why they have to produce a hoop with such violence is a mystery to me when all they have to do is bend over and drop the ball through.

Equally mysterious to me is another phenomenon that has no logical explanation. A team is leading by twenty-three points when, with three minutes left in the game, the opposition comes to life and erases the deficit and wins the game with a long three-point shot with one second left on the clock. If they were so intent on winning, why didn't they play like that all through the game and spare everybody the emotional upheaval that such a finish produces!

On a par with the mysterious nature of the above mentioned items is the inanity of the interviews -- with the players and coaches -- that take place at halftime and after the game. After witnessing several of these deeply penetrating and marvelously enlightening exchanges, it seems evident that to qualify as an interviewer one has to learn by heart the proper questions -- and never deviate from the formula; and to be hired as a coach or signed on as a member of the team, an essential talent is to have the answers imbedded in memory and to give those answers without hesitation or originality.

But, like Martin Luther King, I have a dream, not one as noble and inspiring, but a dream, nonetheless.

I dream of an interview with, for example, a coach who has been cornered at halftime of the game by a breathless and intense reporter, armed with a microphone and all the standard questions, and who gives all the wrong answers.

For the sake of easy identification, we will designate the overzealous questioner with the "I" for "Interviewer" and the one being harassed with the code letters "OBI" for the "One Being Interviewed."

I: "You've done a wonderful job with this team, Coach. To what do you ascribe your phenomenal success?"

OBI: "To the fact that the alumni were able to buy me the tallest and fastest players in the country."

I: "Uh, yes, well, do you intend to follow the same strategy in the second half as you used in the first half?"

OBI: "No, that was too easy. We were too physical in the first half. In this half we are going to be spiritual."

I: "Oh, er, well, you have some boys on this team that are, I'm told, not only superb athletes but excellent students. Your center, for example, has a 3.5 grade point average. Just what is he majoring in?"

OBI: "Basket weaving and bubble gum blowing."

I: "Gulp. So tell me, Coach, why you use the chalkboard so much to teach players. Millions of fans want to know."

OBI: "I have to draw pictures for these guys. Most of them don't know how to read."

I: "Yes, well, do you look forward to a long tenure with this very successful program, Coach?"

OBI: "Gosh, no. I look forward to getting out of this rat race as soon as possible, away from this gang of ill-educated, prima donna players, arrogant, know-it-all alumni, and endless and pointless interviews on TV and radio."

I: "Well, ah, thank you, Coach, for your enlightening remarks, and I'll be looking forward to hearing your analysis of the game after its conclusion … I think."

As you may have noticed, I have only a mild interest in basketball, and I don't really care who wins the NCAA tournament, just so somebody beats the jerseys off of Bobby Knight and his Hoosiers.

The Saga of the Sag

by Father Elstan
May 1993

At this time of the year, in the "old days," my plans for summer vacation used to intensify. I say "intensify" because those plans would begin right after the new year and build up to the time of departure for the lake for two weeks of serious fishing. The planning involved Father Hugolinus, better known as "Hugie," and Father Matt, and, of course, me.

Hugie was the consummate planner. A major element of his enjoyment of our vacation was the planning of it. Within days after the start of the new year, Matt and I received a letter from him urging us to come to an agreement on the date of our departure, "as soon as possible after school lets out," and to let him know immediately.

There was always an air of urgency in these communications because, as he made clear to us, he had to devote the rest of the time till the start of our trip to getting together the list of things we would have to take along.

The list went on forever, containing as it did mostly items we would never need nor use in two weeks at the lake. But Hugie didn't want to overlook any possibility. By the time we gathered to take off, his big Chevrolet was packed up to the ceiling -- and beyond -- with a few items sticking out of the back windows. One year he forgot toothpicks, of all things. Every year from then on, Matt and I, in our planning letters, emphasized toothpicks. Hugie always took us seriously.

One of our favorite destinations was Lake Saganaga, for brevity's sake referred to as "The Sag," which is, as many of you are aware, a large body of water that is half in the Arrowhead area of Minnesota and half in Canada. There are, roughly, three hundred islands in the lake and they all look identical. We only found the right one each year by reason of our keen memories, great feats of navigation, and mostly luck.

The way we came to have access to this glorious spot is worth a paragraph or two.

There was a federal judge in St. Paul -- Judge Hashey, by name -- whose work was stressful and confining. He became quite friendly with Hugie and me when we were stationed together in the '50's on the east side of the city. The judge felt the need for a vacation retreat, far from the madding crowd, remote and rustic. A friend of his told him there were several islands in "The Sag" that the Canadian government was prepared to sell to private investors. They took a trip together to look over the area and test the fishing.

One day when they were out in their boat, soaking up the solitude, and the sun was getting down close to the western horizon, they realized they didn't have a watch along. About that time a bewhiskered and sunburnt old French Canadian trapper in a canoe filled with pelts paddled into view. They hailed him and said, "Hey! What time is it?"

The old guy scratched his flea-bitten head and said, "Time!?#*@! I don't even know what month it is!"

That made up the judge's mind. If anybody could be that indifferent to something that was so much a part of his everyday life, that's what he was looking for. He bought an island -- about five acres -- built a cabin on it, and a dock, and escaped there whenever he could.

One year he invited Hugie and me to go with him. It took us all of five seconds to accept his offer. We returned there year after year, sometimes with the judge, and when he couldn't arrange his time for it, we went alone.

The story will get too long if I go into some of the experiences we had together on "The Sag," so I'll use them as material for next month's installment. So if you can hold your breath that long, look forward to more on "The Saga of the Sag."

Gold Strike on The Sag

by Father Elstan
June 1993

When a narrative such as this is presented to the reading public in bits and pieces over a period of several months, it behooves the chronicler to briefly review that which was already told.

Recall that the location of choice for our annual fishing vacation ("our" being Frs. Matt, Hugie, and I) was an island in the middle of Lake Saganaga off the tip of the Arrowhead of Minnesota. Half of the lake is in the U.S., half in Canada. Our island and cabin were on the Canadian side.

On the way to the island it was necessary for us to pull in to another island that rested astride the U.S.-Canadian border, to go through customs. One year the customs officer was a jovial Canadian lady who, in the course of our bantering back and forth, discovered we were Catholic priests. She immediately showed great interest and asked if we intended to say Mass in our cabins. We said we did.

"Could you manage to say Mass at eight o'clock on Sunday morning?" she asked. We said we could but wished to know why she inquired. She said,

"Because I intend to be there, and there are others on the lake who would like to attend. I'll get a shortwave and get the word out to all the islands and around the shore."

To review a bit, you may remember my mentioning that when Fr. Hugie began to plan for a fishing vacation, he was thorough and complete. Fr. Matt and I had to use our fullest powers of persuasion to prevent him from packing his kitchen sink into the trunk of his Bel-Air before we left home. Among other items, and high on his long list, Fr. H. packed what is called in "the trade" a Mass kit.

Sunday came around and we set up for Mass on a table in the living room. Shortly before eight o'clock there was a respectful tap on the door, which, when opened, revealed a flotilla of boats of all descriptions bearing down on our location. It looked like the invasion of Normandy on D-Day.

There were tourists in outboard motors and sailboats. There were grizzled old Canadian fur trappers in canoes, dressed in their Sunday-go-to-meeting buckskins, moccasins, and coonskin caps, with chins that hadn't been put to a razor since their owners had been born.

They filled our living room and parked on both sides of the dock -- and out into the lake. The trappers removed their caps, spat out their chewing tobacco, and assumed a reverent attitude, and Mass began.

At the Offertory someone in the crowd decided the Mass wasn't valid unless there was a collection, so he picked up his empty minnow bucket and made the rounds. He paddled out to every craft anchored out in the lake, and the congregation felt constrained to make up for all the times they were unable to get to church on Sunday -- and hadn't been able to contribute to the support of their parish. As I recall, the total take was $700. It paid for our entire vacation with an ample amount left over.

But the recollection of that vacation that remains more vivid than the number and size of the fish we caught, or the response at the Offertory, was the silent, reverent attitude of the congregation, sitting in their boats and straining to hear the words of the Mass.

Before we got everything folded up and put away at the end of the celebration, most of the tourists and all of the "Canooks" had faded away into the woods and waterways.

Smile, Aristotle! Smile!

by Father Elstanmik
July 1993

One final visit to Lake Saganaga. You will recall that a Judge Hackey had bought an island in the lake as a place to escape from the pressures of his profession.

In my previous mention of the judge, I spelled his name "Hashey." Well, that's the way it's pronounced, but Jim Larkin, who knew the judge in the exercise of his legal profession, pointed out that I had misspelled the name. I should have known better because the judge had a plaque over the door on the cabin on the island in the lake that read, "Hackey's Hideout."

But none of this is germane to the point I want to make in this space.

We were not the only life forms on the island. Whenever the judge was there, there also was Aristotle, a mystery dog. He seemed to belong to no one, had no visible means of support, and no permanent address. For the judge to name him Aristotle was a cruel jest, for it simply tended to put into sharp relief his monumental ignorance.

In addition to his vast stupidity, Aristotle sported an equal amount of bulk. Somewhere along the line of the evolutionary process, a black bear's genes must have inserted themselves into his family tree. It had to be a black bear because Aristotle was so black the judge had to feed him garlic so he could find him in the dark.

Much of Aristotle's size was concentrated in his tail, which was about the length of his body and weighed about as much as the trunk of a mature northern pine. He used this instrument of destruction to sweep dishes off the table, knock over furniture, and bruise the legs of us who were in the cabin with him.

His tongue is worth comment, too. It was about the size and consistency of a well-soaked bath towel, and it was used mainly to swap people across the face -- whoever got within swatting distance, that is. On one occasion we were sitting around and commenting on Aristotle's ghastly appearance and abysmal ignorance when the judge said, "There's a face of Aristotle that has escaped your notice."

"What," we inquired, "might that be?"

"I'll bet you don't know many dogs that can smile," said he.

"We know of none," was our response.

"Watch this," said the judge. We watched as the judge called Aristotle to attention. "Smile, Aristotle! Smile!"

Aristotle braced his four huge legs, threw his mammoth head in the air, and began to tense every muscle. The expression on his face showed intense concentration. It looked as though he were about to give birth to the Antichrist.

Once more the judge urged: "Smile, Aristotle! Smile!" And a broad and beautiful smile suffused his ugly features. He held it for a while -- with what was obviously a colossal effort -- and for a brief moment the cabin lit up, birds ceased their song, and all nature paused to witness the spectacle.

When he released the smile, Aristotle melted into a heap. He was completely spent by the effort, and he wasn't available for interview till late the next morning.

A Scene from Hell

by Father Elstan
August 1993

If I were a betting man, which I am not, except for sums not exceeding 25 cents, I would hazard a wager that many of your memories revolve around "firsts" in your life -- the first major league game you ever saw, the first time you heard of the Kennedy assassination, your First Communion, your first day in school, your first movie.

The memory of my first movie is so indelibly imprinted on my mind it might have been put there with a branding iron. Some background is necessary to explain why this is so.

I was four years old. There was a parish mission in progress at our church in Jordan. For those of you who don't know, or have forgotten, a parish mission in those days was on a par in excitement and attendance with the county fair -- and a baseball game between Jordan and the dreaded enemy, Shakopee.

Everybody went. All other activities were suspended during the time of the mission. My parents, of course, attended the mission every evening. My sister, my senior by two years, and my inveterate nemesis, was taken along one evening while I had to stay home with the baby sitter.

After the evening sermon and service, the folks met up with some friends of theirs and took in the movie -- in those days referred to as the "moving picture show" -- and when alluded to by us kids was constructed to sound like "moom pitcher show." My smart aleck sister got to see the movie.

Things had been getting a little out of hand about this time. This obnoxious woman had just recently gotten to lick out the frosting bowl when my mom made a cake. "Nah, nah, nah, nah, nah, nah!" She was going to start school in the fall and I had to stay home. "Nah, nah, nah, nah, nah, nah!" And now this. "I got to go to the moom pitcher show and you didn't! Hah! Hah! Hah!"

Drastic action was called for. This kind of persecution had to stop. I wasn't quite sure what a moom pitcher show was nor what it was like, but from my sister's description of it I could tell it was the experience of a lifetime. I decided I had to get my mom and dad to take me along the next evening when they went to church and drop me off at the theater.

The first showing started about the same time as the mission service. I kicked up so much sand and raised such a hew and cry that my progenitor finally relented and promised to deposit me in the theater and pick me up outside it after the mission and about the time the show would let out. They made clear to me that it was a scary show; I would be all alone; it would be dark in the theater; and could I assure them I wouldn't be scared.

"Scared? Me? Huh!" The thought was ludicrous.

The time for the great adventure arrived. Mom and Dad led me down the aisle of the cavernous building to a seat close to the front, and then abandoned me. The lights went out and the movie started, "All Quiet on the Western Front." Presently the shooting started and I was certain that if the Armageddon wasn't in progress, my premature demise certainly was.

In one scene a tough looking soldier aimed his submachine gun directly at me, and my whole sinful life flashed before my eyes. I ducked down behind the seat in front of me and commended my immortal soul to God. There was a glowing red light just to the right of where I was sitting and sweating, and I would have followed its direction without hesitation if I had been able to read -- and know what "exit" meant.

Eventually the war ended, and I was the first one out of the theater -- even though I was seated farther from the door than anybody else.

There have been times in my life subsequently when I have been happy to see someone waiting for me, but at no time have I ever been happier than when I saw Mom and Dad waiting for me outside of that scene from hell. I was questioned carefully by my parents, and the next day by my sister, about how scared I had been. I flatly denied being frightened at all. We guys who had been through a war don't scare easily.

Friars Test the Insurance Agent

by Father Elstan
September 1993

There is rarely anything funny about a car accident. Somebody usually gets hurt -- or worse -- and among those affected is the insurance company and the agent who represents it. He or she has to respond to your claims and hope the number of your misfortunes while driving are held to a bare minimum.

It was the winter of '59. I was stationed at Sacred Heart in St. Paul with Father Hugolinus, the pastor; Father Reginald, the second assistant; and Father Theodore, the third assistant who has no bearing on this narrative since he couldn't drive anyway. It was the last week in December, one of the times available for an annual retreat.

Fr. Hugolinus (sometimes known to us as Fr. Hugo, occasionally receiving correspondence addressed to "Fr. Hugo Linus," now and then even "Huge O'Line") had just gotten a new Chevy at Christmas and decided to make his retreat in Chicago over the new year lull and, as it were, break in his big black car in the process.

The day before New Year's Eve, he -- Hugie -- and a friend of his, after the evening conference, drove into the city to visit his -- Hugie's -- sister and show off his new car.

When they pulled into the yard at the retreat house, the car stalled, then stopped. As they were getting out of the car it burst into flames, and before they got the fire department on the scene and the conflagration extinguished, the function of the car's engine had been rendered null and void.

The next morning Fr. H. called me, described the incident with well chosen adjectives and asked me to call our insurance agent the next morning.

Jack Davis, for such was his name, was a mild-mannered man and very accommodating. He took the news well and advised me to call Fr. H. and have him get the necessary repairs made, and to bring the bills back with him for verification.

New Year's Day, after the morning Masses, I drove out to the farm near Jordan to spend the holiday with my mother and whoever else of the clan would congregate there. About the time supper was over, it began to sleet a bit. I decided to head back for the city. By the time I got on the highway, the road surface was like that of a well maintained skating rink. I crept along at about five mph.

Suddenly, an eighteen-wheeler going in the opposite direction loomed up over a hill. He was driving from the north where the storm had not yet reached.

He hit the ice, then hit the brakes and began to spin. I remember thinking, "That guy's in trouble."

Then he began to spin across the median and headed straight for me. I thought, "I'm in trouble." I was. The back of his truck hit the front of my car and practically cut the motor in half.

The next morning I called Hugie, who had the decency to ask if I had been hurt. I hadn't. Then he said, "Well, call Jack and tell him what happened." I called Jack and told him what happened. He was nice about it.

The next day Fr. Reginald was downtown in St. Paul when he skidded into a light pole. He called and described the damage and asked me to call Jack -- good old Jack. I said, "Sure. No problem. I know his number by heart."

Jack was heroically patient, mentioned that "you guys are having a run of bad luck" -- which I knew already -- and made the suggestion that we be sure to drive carefully.

The next day Hugie came home -- his car fixed and functioning -- but when I stepped outside to help him carry in his luggage I noticed a dent running the full length of the car, and the paint scraped off.

I asked the obvious question: "What happened?" He had pulled into a convenience store and the person parked next to him backed out, turned too sharply, and did the damage.

After describing the incident he said, "Will you call Jack Davis and tell him what happened?" Without hesitation I said, "No! I won't! If he hears my voice one more time within the next ten years he will snap pencils between his fingers, start to stick straws in his hair, and might even run off and join the French Foreign Legion. You call him and tell him or, better yet, let's not tell him at all and just have the blooming thing repaired on our own."

Hugie called him, and a few days later Jack got in touch with his medical insurance agent. It was a bad case of ulcers.

Introducing Avery Wright

by Father Elstan
October 1993

Somebody should put on permanent record the exploits and adventures of Avery Wright. I propose to do that.

I met him outside of the bank in Harbor Springs in 1967 -- a most gregarious individual. He knew about our operation of an Indian boarding school and admired the work of the Notre Dame Sisters who trained, taught, and disciplined the 120 little Ottawas who lived at the school throughout the year.

His admiration expressed itself in his unobtrusively providing a complete meal for each of the kids and all of us connected with the school every year at Thanksgiving time.

He invited me to have supper with him at his home "on top of the bluff" above the town the following Wednesday, and to meet his wife Donna. That started a regular practice which lasted the entire time of my stint in Harbor Springs -- six years.

A most striking feature of his home, besides his wife, was the kitchen. The two walls enclosing the area were full of shelves which, in turn, were full of volumes, all of which were cookbooks from every corner of the world.

Avery had become an accomplished gourmet cook and, in all the meals I had with him over those years, I don't recall him ever repeating the same meal twice. If the recipe originated from some obscure section of the world and the ingredients were not available in the U.S., he simply improvised. Rarely did that happen, though, for he seemed to have connections everywhere.

Of more interest, however, than his culinary triumphs were the wild tales of his life's adventures, including both successes and failures.

Avery's dad owned the milk bottle division of the Corning Glass Company. For years, that put him on a secure financial basis and made it possible for him to send his son to an exclusive prep school -- in New Jersey, I think. The prep school is named Lawrenceville.

Avery didn't exactly set a standard for scholastic excellence while in Lawrenceville, relying more on his father's influence than his own efforts to make passing grades.

But, by his own efforts, he did set one standard. In his third year at prep school he set the school record for the 400-meter dash -- a record that still held at the time of his telling me about it fifty-some years later.

About that time the First World War broke out (the war Avery always insisted on referring to as "the big one"), and he couldn't sit still. Having accomplished all he could at Lawrenceville with his 400-meter dash record, he walked out of the place and went to join the Air Corps. He was rejected. The recruiting officer questioned his age, and subsequent investigation proved his questioning justified.

Avery headed for Canada, where, apparently, those who recruited did so with one eye closed to age requirements; and so, at the age 17 -- officially 18 -- Avery became a member of the Royal Canadian Air Force.

He landed in England where he seems to have used his flying skill mainly for the purpose of staying out of range and sight of the Red Baron and his crowd. So he easily survived the war.

There is more to Avery than the above, and I'll expand on that next month.

Avery and the London Bridge

by Father Elstan
November 1993

If you will cast your memory back to last month's *Gazette*, you will recall you were introduced to Mr. Avery Wright of Harbor Springs, Michigan. We left him in England where he had served in the Royal Canadian Air Force. When flying missions over enemy territory, he made it a priority to stay out of sight of Kaiser Wilhelm's cadets, and so survived the war.

He was hanging around London waiting for his honorable discharge, and while waiting he made it his business to raise the eyebrows of the staid citizenry of the metropolis. According to his descriptions of escapades with his fellow pilots, London would have welcomed his prompt discharge -- honorable or otherwise -- and his return to the home of his birth.

One day a buddy of his and he were hanging around a London bridge, leaning over the railing, watching the historic Thames flow by below, and discussing life's mysteries and remarking how boring their present existence was.

Suddenly, as if by divine inspiration, his buddy said, "Avery, I'll bet you fifty American dollars you can't fly under this bridge." Avery looked carefully at the available flying space between the bridge and the water -- and took the bet.

His first problem was to acquire a plane. He went to his airstrip and conned a machine out of the attendants -- some wild story about a general needing to be picked up and brought back to the city.

He flew out over the historic bridge, circled it a few times, and came in straight and true. He zoomed under the bridge without incident and flew back to the airstrip, fully convinced that all had gone well and he was about to collect fifty big ones from the one who dared him to do it.

When he hopped out of his plane he was met by his C.O. who was standing on the bridge when Avery flew under it. He took a jaundiced view of Avery's efforts. In fact, as he was painting a vivid and unpleasant picture to Avery of his immediate future, veins stood out on his neck and a purple hue suffused his contorted face.

He led Avery away in chains, and the ensuing court-martial resulted in our hero being sent to the north of England where he spent six months as a guest of her majesty's government in the British equivalent of the Bastille.

During this relatively quiet period in Avery's life, his dad back home was pulling the necessary strings and greasing the right palms to get his boy out of the stir and bring him back to the bosom of his family and the land of his birth.

Avery was reluctant to leave England till he could find his friend and collect his hard-earned fifty -- but wiser heads prevailed, and he returned. Back in the States he became restless and joined one of the barnstorming groups that flew around the country giving flying exhibitions and rides to people at state fairs and other events where admiring crowds oohed and aahed and opened up their purses.

Eventually, after too many close calls, and with a conviction that there was a safer and more lucrative way of putting bread on the table, he left the barnstorming business and went into something else, which will be discussed at length in next month's installment.

Avery, a Man of Magic

by Father Elstan
December 1993

We left our soldier of fortune, Avery Wright, just as he left the barnstorming business for safer pursuits.

He wound up in California where he met Walt Disney and another man, whose name I can't remember, and formed a partnership. Somehow they had access to a geological survey that indicated -- correctly, as history has proven -- that there were large oil deposits under the north slope in Alaska's Prudhoe Bay. They rounded up ten million dollars to finance the drillings. I suspect Avery's share came largely from the generosity of his dad.

The adventure was a washout. Before they ran into oil they ran out of money, and came back to the more clement climate of California.

About this time an opportunity presented itself to Avery to acquire a huge supply of contraband Scotch whiskey. He made use of the opportunity and made a killing. Again, I suspect this adventure was financed by his father.

While tooling around California, and reaping the benefits of his investment in smuggled Scotch whiskey, he met Donna Winslow. In the year 1922 she was listed -- by those who list such things -- as one of ten most beautiful women in the country -- or world. I don't recall which.

Her father owned the milk bottle division of the Pittsburg Glass Company, a healthy source of income in those days. They married and became parents of four sturdy sons.

Life in California was a constant picnic for them, to hear them tell it. They moved in the most exclusive circles of the stars of that era. Errol Flynn had them grace his yacht frequently; they hung around with Clark Gable; and some of the big producers of movies attempted to talk Donna into acting. She knew that was not for her, and Avery vetoed the schemes, too.

Eventually too many of the big names showed too much interest in her, and both she and Avery felt it right to move on -- to, of all places, Toledo, Ohio. I think there was some factory there that was tied to their interests in glass.

I believe it was in Toledo, or sometime during his years in Toledo, that he met the famous magician, Harry Houdini. Magic fascinated Avery, and he studied under Houdini, eventually becoming so proficient he was accepted into a very exclusive magicians' club.

By the time I met Avery he was stiffened up too much by arthritis to be able to pull off some of the more spectacular stunts, but he was still superb with the standard stuff and, being the ham that he was, delighted in entertaining his guests, of which he always had many, with his slight-of-hand routines.

His hospitality manifested itself at Avery's house most spectacularly during the Christmas season which, for Avery, started at Thanksgiving and didn't taper off till long after New Year's Eve. The concept of Advent completely escaped him and, for him, it was more a time of merriment than one of meditation and preparation.

May your Christmas be merry because you have prepared by thoughtful prayer -- and contemplation of its true significance.

The Bluff and Bravado of Avery

by Father Elstan
January 1994

To continue the delineation of Avery Wright's colorful character, I preface this presentation with the remark that he never met a challenge he didn't like.

His athletic bent put him on skis on a regular basis when he was in his prime. On one occasion he was attending a rather prestigious ski jump competition. He was not one of the competitors but managed -- by bluff, bravado, and a degree of luck -- to insert himself into the lineup between two legitimate contestants.

While the announcers were frantically searching their schedules for a name, and conferring with each other and asking some penetrating questions, Avery took off down the ski run. He executed the run flawlessly, performed the jump in a professional manner, landed gracefully, and then, while making his approach to the end of the run, fell down ungloriously.

He was surrounded by officials before he could shake the snow out of his costume and was subjected to more intense interrogation. The result was he was banned from all future competition.

Avery's golf game was excellent. One year, by using influence in high places, he got himself placed on the roster of the Augusta Open, the Masters. In those days it was a Pro-Am event.

On the first hole at the beginning of the tournament, he got off a towering drive. With the aid of a tail wind, and a one-in-a-hundred chance of hitting a rock that was slanted toward the hole, and a good roll, he came to rest within an easy chip shot to the green.

He negotiated that with ease, placing the ball so close to the hole it was a "gimme." He had eagled the par five opening hole and sent shock waves through the ranks of all present, especially the professionals. But his game fell to pieces after that, and he finished well down in the standings, possibly even last, if I caught the gist of his narrative.

At the age of 75, Avery realized there was one adventure he had not yet experienced. He had never owned a motorcycle. He filled that void in his life by investing in a state of the art Harley Davidson. He purchased a leather jacket and a helmet and gloves and for one whole summer kept the local gentry on pins and needles and the medical clinics on alert.

He rarely ventured out on the roads of Emmett County on his high-powered transportation without some incident to narrate upon his return. By the end of the summer he was persuaded to sell his Harley, dispose of his leather jacket, which he gave to me and which I have held onto to this day. I'm not sure why I've kept it. I never wear it, but it is kind of a symbol of Avery's enduring zest for life, and in a way describes who he was.

At this time of year Avery and Donna always threw some memorable parties to celebrate the New Year. I can't throw a party for you, but I can tell you I sincerely wish for you all God's best blessings throughout 1994.

Avery's Anger at the Colonial Inn

by Father Elstan
February 1994

One last effort to present a better picture of Avery Wright's colorful personality -- by way of anecdote.

Harbor Springs, Michigan, where I was stationed at the time the following events transpired, was a favorite vacation spot for the rich and famous as well as the humblest of Franciscan friars. About a half a dozen of the latter had gathered there one summer for fun and frolic, and Avery heard about their presence. He immediately assumed the position of an official one-man entertainment committee.

He arranged a day of golf for us at a course in the area that was so exclusive the governor of the state had been refused membership on the basis of having been heard using a double negative in a political speech one time.

Following the afternoon of golf, it was planned for us to meet Avery at the Colonial Inn for supper -- Oh, excuse me, "dinner." I can only give you an idea of how exclusive this eating place was by mentioning that there were those who were members of the golf club which we had just played who were refused entrance at the Colonial Inn.

We donned slacks and sport shirts and drove up the curved driveway at the Colonial Inn. We were met by several young men, one of whom took the car keys in a white-gloved hand; one attended the door of the car; one stood by to help us alight from the car -- and on and on.

They all seemed to have a stunned expression as they looked back and forth at each other and at us like they were witnessing a disaster in progress. We ignored their problems and walked to a massive and richly carved door of the establishment, in front of which stood an imposing figure -- massive in proportions and attired in medals, braids, epaulets, a crown of some sort, and an expression on his face of offended dignity.

We told him we were Avery's guests. He was unimpressed. He stared past us into the setting sun as he informed us in well chosen words and a nicely modulated voice that we were improperly attired for the Colonial Inn and could not be admitted.

About this time Avery poked his head out the door and picked up the drift of the conversation. He immediately became vocal, using words and phrases you might expect to hear from a group of sailors on shore leave, but the "King of Azer Bai Darn" remained adamant, pointing out that he had a serious responsibility to maintain the high standards of the Colonial Inn.

Things were getting tense, so we told Avery we would go home and change. We were only about a half mile from the Inn. We didn't have a clue where we were going to find the "proper attire" referred to by "his majesty" in tones of great reverence.

As we drove toward the monastery, one of the group remembered that clerical attire is always proper for any occasion or location. We donned Roman collars and returned. The expression on the faces of the team that met our car had changed dramatically; and when we approached the major-domo, his lower jaw dropped down to his chest, his eyes protruded in a marked manner, and he deflated like a punctured balloon.

He became apologetic and almost friendly, and led us in solemn procession into the sacred precincts, where Avery was still kicking up a lot of sand and threatening the manager with canceling his membership. A few words of explanation from the potentate soothed things down somewhat but, although the evening was pleasant and, in general, successful, Avery remained belligerent and vocal until he downed a tall scotch and water.

There was never a dull moment when Avery was around. Even arguing with him was an adventure -- and we argued a lot -- but that never lessened his reverence and respect for the clergy. Much of our arguing centered around theological topics, and we were worlds apart on those subjects. I think he was searching for truth, and I like to think he has found it.

My Mother at the Speedway

by Father Elstan
March 1994

In the final bit on the subject of Avery Wright, and his unorthodox lifestyle, I alluded to his casual pursuit of truth in the area of religion. It seems that there are a large number of people who ponder, with some degree of intensity or another, the profound questions about our existence and its purpose.

This fact becomes evident when a clergyman appears in a Roman collar. Inevitably, some stranger presents himself to ask, "Could the Pope get married if he wanted to?" or "What if one of the candles should go out during Mass?" or something equally demanding of a definite answer.

It was just such a need for truth that led a young woman years ago, when I was stationed in Chaska, to come along to investigate the religion of her husband. We began instructions with her. As the instructions progressed, she mentioned she had a friend who was anxious to join her in class, and the three of us met weekly and plowed through the adult catechism together.

In time it came out in casual conversation that their husbands, for diversion on Sunday afternoon, drove racecars at the newly opened Raceway Park (I think that's the name) near Savage; and that they, too -- these fragile young mothers -- drove cars around the same track once a week in what was appropriately called the "powder puff derby."

I exhibited mild interest in their and their husband's diversion, and they presented me with a ticket one day -- which I used the following Sunday.

The track was in a primitive state of development at the time, with a dirt surface and open bleachers for the spectators. I enjoyed the spectacle very much, especially the powder puff derby in which my friends drove off the track, into each other, across the infield, and, on a couple of occasions, almost into the grandstand.

The day's activities also featured a demolition derby in which the men drove, which could scarcely be distinguished from the feminine approach to racing.

I told my mother about my experience at the race track, and she wondered aloud if I could take her out to witness the races some day. I was surprised at her interest -- but I guess I shouldn't have been.

When it came to driving, Mom's main intent was to get from Point A to Point B in as little time as possible. For her, the speed limit sign (which in those days was 45 mph, I believe) was merely a suggested speed, and was meant mainly for those who were in less of a hurry than she. When she drove to church on Sunday, I don't ever recall coming late.

When Dad drove, on the other hand, he considered the car as deserving of a day of rest, too, and didn't push it very hard. Anytime he got behind the wheel he considered himself on a leisurely vacation and kept the speed down to where he could drive and at the same time observe his neighbors' crops and cattle, and if the neighbors were out in the yard he could carry on quite a lengthy conversation as he drove past. His interpretation of the speed limit was that the more you drove under the limit, the more law-abiding you were.

But I digress. Mom and I went out to the speedway. She was thrilled, and I think during the powder puff derby she imagined herself driving one of those open-air, battered up frames on wheels. I heard her occasionally emit a dignified squeal of excitement, and she even went so far as to say at various intervals -- "Mercy!" "My goodness!" "Go, girls, go!" "Watch out, dear!" and similar appropriate remarks.

There was no way around it. I had to bring her to the races again. This time it was a hot and windy day in August. The brisk breeze was from the east. We were in the grandstand on the west side. The racers kicked up a prodigious amount of dust, all of which blew over and settled on us.

Mom was so embarrassed at her appearance by the time we drove home, she hunkered down behind the dashboard so as to escape the eye of any who might glance into the car.

We never went back to the speedway. Mom followed the races in the newspaper after that. When I asked her if she wanted to go back, she said she thought it was rather a silly pastime for a mature woman to indulge in -- and for a priest, too, for all that.

The Heroic Rescue of Maude

by Father Elstan
April 1994

Periodically it seems proper to present a chapter in the life of my toy dachshund, Maude -- a life lived on the cutting edge, a life replete with drama, danger, and derring-do.

It was one of those days in our recent Siberian winter. It had snowed generously during the night, and early in the morning Joe Michel had plowed the parking lot open and deposited a mini-mountain of precipitation along the front of the Parish Center.

I opened my door and Maude streaked out. (Considering her lack of covering, I use the term "streak" not only to describe the speed with which she ran, but also the nude condition in which she ran.)

In the middle of the parking lot loitered a cat of mammoth proportions. At first glance I thought it was a cat whose ancestors had gotten crossed with a grizzly bear somewhere along the line. In addition to a generous coat of hair over rippling muscles, it had an inflated head, and paws the size of one of our Lions Club pancakes.

Maude's wolf genes asserted themselves and she undertook to defend her territory. Her lips curled back in a nasty scowl, her hair rose on her back menacingly, and her bark made it clear she meant business. Pursuit ensued.

The cat -- if that's what it was -- was unimpressed. He sauntered out on top of the pile of snow, stopped and turned around, and watched as Maude plunged in after him, and stood there with a nasty grin on his ugly face as he observed Maude sink out of sight.

I observed it all with horror. Maude's black-button nose appeared on the surface at intervals -- in the same spot -- and with the intervals between appearances coming further apart as time went on. She was making no progress horizontally, and less and less vertically.

My course of action became clear. With no thought for my own comfort and convenience -- and, I might almost say, safety -- and with a heroism of which I scarcely thought myself capable, I plunged in and dug with my bare hands on the spot where Maude's nose had last appeared.

I finally reached where she was cowering in a terrified, cold, and exhausted condition. I shook the snow off her and carried her into the house where she immediately curled up in front of the heat vent, and where she stayed the rest of the day.

I recall this drama because it is the time to celebrate the events of Holy Week; and it occurred to me that Maude experienced Good Friday and the Resurrection all within the space of twenty minutes -- and some weeks prematurely.

May you experience Resurrection joy and peace at this time.

Gramma and Her Code of Etiquette

by Father Elstan
May 1994

After using an incident in the life of my paternal grandmother in a homily lately, I find myself recalling other events from the years she spent with our immediate family -- lasting till 1936 -- that led to a profound distaste for her standards of ethics and etiquette in my brother and me.

Grandma adhered to the conviction that since she had descended from high church Episcopalian ancestry, she was the proper guardian of our speech and physical cleanliness. Any word from us that was more colorful or descriptive than "pshaw!" met with an immediate and negative reaction from her. Any appearance at table with our hair uncombed, a bit of loam under our fingernails, some dust in our ears, or one suspender unhooked or missing prompted her to put on an act of near-swooning. If we were on our way to church, the standard in these areas went up a notch.

"Gramma" held up to us as an example to emulate a beastly brother of hers who had become a preacher -- Presbyterian, I think -- and who had gone out to the western frontier to confront the evils in that pioneer society. She never tired of telling us that he had returned from that unsensory atmosphere without succumbing in the slightest to its lax speech patterns, its casual dress code, and its nonexistent refinements.

I remember thinking -- but not expressing within earshot of Gramma -- "Well, bully for him!" My brother concurred in that sentiment. We developed an intense dislike for that saintly man, even though we never met him.

There were a couple of Gramma's practices we could relate to with ease even though we always suspected her motives were bribery rather than sweet charity.

Every Sunday, after church, we had to stop at the store and get a supply of ginger ale. According to Gramma's judgment, that was the preferred drink of the aristocracy, and nothing inferior to it was good enough for her. We all got our ration of her elixir, and fortunately we all liked it because we would have had to drink it even if we didn't.

In addition to the above example, she had another way of bringing our loyalty to her high standards. She had a rocking chair that was equipped with a drawer on a pivot under the seat. She kept a supply of white candy mints in the drawer which she doled out to us at proper intervals.

The intervals were too far spaced for our taste, so Jesse and I helped ourselves whenever it could be done without being apprehended. But, of course, she knew who was responsible for the rapid depletion of her supply. Girls would never do such a thing; and since boys were by nature predisposed to thievery, the finger of guilt pointed directly at us. And the manner in which she pointed, and the wording that accompanied the pointing, left no doubt that she considered us future highly-regarded members of the Dalton gang.

Gramma went to glory in 1936 to get things in proper order up there. By the time we join her, everybody present will be speaking the queen's English, be attired in regulation halos and wings, and be observing the strictest code of etiquette -- and will probably be getting a slug of ginger ale and a white candy mint, at tasteful intervals, from her benevolent hand.

Hootin' Tootin' Threshing Machine

by Father Elstan
June 1994

When Father Bernardine was here for a visit several weeks ago, Willie and Jean Bongard put on a dinner party for him and a number of his friends from the days when he was stationed here. Willie showed off his collection of miniature tractors -- and other farm implements, including an old grain separator. Suddenly I was transported back sixty to sixty-five years ago.

The summer always had its highlights -- the Sunday we journeyed to Glencoe to visit Uncle Frank and Aunt Mayme and their kids; the annual hegira to Uncle Leo and Aunt Sophie and their kids' farm in Young America; the summer visit of Aunt Charlie and Aunt Bessie and their girls, Betty and Patsy; the Fourth of July picnic; the Scott County Fair -- but none of these memorable events came close to the anticipation and excitement engendered in us kids by the arrival of the threshing rig and its entourage.

What awe that locomotive inspired with its wheels large enough to crush "an elephant" -- if one had been so rash as to happen along and get under them. And the flywheel -- big enough for a kid to stand in, given the opportunity. And the smoke stack reaching up halfway to the sun! And the whistle! We heard it toot long before the machine hove into view around the bend of the road, and then another ceremonial snort as it entered the yard.

Each year we revived rumors about locomotives that size that were used on the plains of Alberta and Saskatchewan, Canada (wherever that was), to pull a 16-bottom plow -- and that one like it blew up once and wiped out all the buildings and all forms of life throughout an entire county.

This last hint of danger was kept alive by several of the more imaginative members of the crew -- to keep us out from under their feet. It didn't work. It did add to the excitement.

Then there was the grain separator. What a monument to man's genius -- to build a machine that would carry a bundle into its bowels and spit out straw through one pipe and the grain out of another.

There was the water tank on wheels, hauled by a big pair of Belgian horses and driven by a guy who drifted into the neighborhood every year at harvest time. Several times a day during the threshing run, we kids rode with him down to the creek (or "krick" in kids' talk), where he backed up to the water, scooped out a depression in the creek bed and dropped in a large hose leading to the tank. This was the guy's sacred trust, but the sacredness of that trust was not sufficiently appreciated by us kids.

While he was pumping water, we were running up and down the stream kicking up mud, sand, stones, and various kinds of vegetation. This material could not be used in the boiler of the steam engine -- and we were told so in language that was hardly appropriate for ears so young and tender.

The legendary thresher meals made this annual event unprecedented in the annals of our youth -- as did the conversation of the men as they scrubbed up outside before going in to consume the meals. And remember how the "young turks" who manned the wagons for hauling bundles from the field to the rig -- how, after supper, they would spring up on the hayrack and, like charioteers, bring their teams to a gallop as they headed home for the night?

There were characters that accompanied the threshing run who deserve honorable mention and I will introduce them to you next month.

Hank, Hubie, Louie, and Shorty

by Father Elstan
July 1994

I believe I suggested in last month's "effort" that I would acquaint you with some of the characters that the annual threshing run attracted.

Head and shoulders above all others -- in the eyes of us kids -- was Hank, who maneuvered the mighty steam engine. The fact that he stood at his post behind the wheel in his greasy overalls, black leather cap, and oversized sunglasses -- and, oh yes, high-topped boots -- anointed him with an air of power and complete control.

And his stock with us boys rose at least 20% when he hoisted us up on the platform of his "throne room" and allowed us to ride down the road and through the yard to the location where the real action took place. He even allowed us to pull the chain that blew the whistle that announced our arrival, a privilege that was granted to very few of the elect.

Then there was "Hubie" Stier, the separator man. His responsibility was to perch on a piece of canvas strung between two metal posts on top of the rig and monitor the functioning of the machine when it was in operation

Hubie was of massive proportions, and an unusual amount of his mass had settled in the area of his hind pockets. He fit snugly on his perch. Also massive was his temper, so we kids stayed clear of him and waited for the inevitable, which was as follows …

As the afternoon wore on and the heat of the day and the throbbing of the machinery took its effect, Hubie nodded on his perch, oblivious of events around him. At this juncture, a couple of the spirited young bachelors tossing bundles into the thresher from opposite sides winked at each other and deliberately jammed the machine by overloading it. That afforded everybody the opportunity to recline in the shade with a tall, cool one while Hubie cleaned out the hopper -- and fumed and threatened and taught us kids some additional vocabulary.

Then there were "Louie Lears" and "Shorty Frank Smith," who followed the harvest from Texas to Saskatchewan. They were both mysterious characters, seeming to have no roots nor family and appeared to be part of the equipment of the threshing run.

Louie had one tooth in his generally glum appearing face. He spoke little and listened less. His job was to drive the wagon that took the grain from the machine to the granary. He also prowled around the whole operation and did odd jobs -- cleaning up spilled bundles of grain, oiling the machinery, moving the straw spout to create a neat pile, etc.

And he entertained a violent dislike for Shorty Frank. On one occasion I remember him taking after Shorty with a neck yoke from a discarded harness.

And Shorty Frank's person and past were always shrouded in mystery. Rumors always persisted when he appeared on the scene that "Shorty Frank Smith" was an assumed name -- used for the purpose of helping him keep ahead of some law enforcement agency down in Texas who was interested in questioning him about a murder that occurred down there in the past. No one on the crew ever questioned him. It wouldn't have done any good, for he was introspective and incommunicative.

What was clear about him was his assigned task, which was to haul the water from, in our case, the creek to the steam engine. It was also clear that he had a monumental appetite for food and Jim Beam.

He also had an abiding aversion to Louie Lears that matched Louie's aversion to him. It was during one of their confrontations that Louie adverted to the incident in Texas -- which prompted Shorty to assume a new identity.

These two supplied us boys with a topic of conversation and speculation for many days after the job was finished on our farm and the parade -- of Hank and his steam engine, Hubie and his separator, Shorty and his water tank, and the seven or eight teams, and Louie on foot -- pulled out of the yard to perform the same routine at the neighbor's place.

It was always like the final act of a great drama for us kids -- the time when the threshers were finished and departed.

Exaggerated History

by Father Elstan
August 1994

Sometime, around the Fourth of July, a nondescript group of us got to talking about the errors and exaggerations that have crept into our American history, especially in connection with our national heroes.

One of the group pointed out that the story of George Washington throwing a silver dollar across the Potomac River was transparently false. It is physically impossible for anyone to throw a silver dollar -- or anything else -- that far. Black Jack McDowell couldn't do it. Roger Clements couldn't do it. And any Twins pitcher who tried it would probably have thrown it in the wrong direction.

(One Weisenheimer in the group had to revive the old observation that a dollar went a lot further in those days, of course.)

Someone pointed out that the story of George chopping down a cherry tree, and then, in the interest of honesty, admitted to his dad that he was the one who perpetrated the dastardly deed, was highly suspect.

Many of the stories that surround the life of Lincoln are very likely apocryphal too. Did he actually use the back of a shovel and a piece of charcoal as his writing materials when he was studying his arithmetic? Who honestly believes that he walked barefoot many miles after dark to return two cents to a storekeeper that he owed?

The exploits of Jack Kennedy during his stint in the navy during World War II will be a part of the story of his life from now on, when these stories are only the result of the fertile imagination of the MGM scriptwriter.

In the course of the conversation, I interjected the observation that these kinds of distortions have crept into the lives of the saints as well. St. Patrick's life has spawned its share of unbelievable anecdotes. In addition to the fact that he is reported to have driven the snakes out of Ireland -- and there aren't any there -- there were reports of him standing up to his neck in ice-cold water. One report is that he stayed there for eight hours every morning in deep prayer -- another that he spent eight hours in that altitude through the afternoon -- and another that he spent ten hours through the night in that manner. That's a total of 26 hours in one day. Come now! Unless he could stop the sun for two hours every day, and he was immune to hypothermia, I don't think so.

St. Anthony's life gave rise to a plethora of imaginary events. One that can't be substantiated historically is that he was preaching to a crowd of people on the shore of a lake, and the people wouldn't pay any attention -- so he turned to the lake and preached to the fish, who stuck their heads out of the water and listened in wrapped attention till he concluded his remarks. I assume they took his word to heart and went back to their home and families, reformed in mind and renewed in spirit.

When he was a young man, his father is supposed to have asked him to stay out in the field and shoo the birds away to keep them from eating the freshly planted seeds ... There was a small rural church nearby that strongly attracted St. Anthony to come and pray. He invited the birds to come along. They did. Eventually the dad came out to the field and, in a huff, looked for his son. He found him in ecstasy with the birds all sitting in reverent attention. It's possible, ... but I don't know.

Stories of this kind are interwoven into the lives of most of the saints, especially those who go far back into history. It's all right. These anecdotes help to identify who they were -- like a good novel about a real person, or a good movie about a great historic event.

Calls from Blanche and Mary

by Father Elstan
September 1994

My reminiscences in this space a couple of months ago about the annual summer celebration known as "threshing time" elicited a call from my sister Blanche and my sister Mary.

Blanche, in her no-nonsense school-marm manner, reminded me that we boys were not the only ones involved in the threshing operation. I was vaguely aware of all the fuss and furor going on in the kitchen but had forgotten about the clean up after the big black steam engine pulled out of the yard to go to the next location.

Before departing, Hank, the driver of that mighty chariot, always opened up some trapdoor in the rig and dumped the ashes that had accumulated during its stay -- precisely in the middle of the driveway. It fell to Blanche and Mary to clean it up. Why my brother and I escaped that duty, I'm not sure. Possibly because we were too busy hooking a ride on one of the hayracks or the water tank -- or the steam engine.

Anyway, the girls had to make sure the job was thorough, meaning there could not be a trace left of any sharp objects -- spikes, nails, wire. It was Blanche's annual anger day. "I could have just swatted that darn Hank!" "He always made me so mad!" "Why did he always have to dump that stuff in the middle of the driveway?"

I maintained a discreet silence throughout her expressions of indignation at this gross injustice that has persisted for sixty-plus years.

Mary reminded me of the scene that was a standard before each meal, and of the girls' part in setting up for the event. They -- the girls -- had the job of placing a long bench under the giant oak tree outside of the kitchen where a mirror of sorts was tacked to the tree trunk. Huge containers full of hot water waited for the men along with big rough towels and homemade soap designed to remove the deeply embedded dirt by the simple expedient of removing the skin along with the dirt.

The men made a pass at combing their hair by running their wet hands through it until they looked like drowned rats. The whole operation, of course, was accompanied by crude humor and a good deal of juvenile horseplay.

Mary reminded me of something else from those days, but you'll just have to hold your breath till later.

My Dad and Effie the Salesman

by Father Elstan
October 1994

I warned you about this in last month's column. In a conversation with my sister Mary, in which we were discussing the threshing run in the "old days," we branched out into some unrelated recollections.

One of these was about how the old dad took a fiendish delight in flaunting his less than sanitary appearance before the assortment of salesmen and county agents that came by in the course of a day. They were always antiseptically clean and nattily attired. He, by contrast, always looked like he had just emerged from a hog wrestle.

Dirt, grease, and grime seemed to be the natural accompaniment of farmers in those days and, in the case of Dad, more natural than most. His approach was to grasp their well-scrubbed hand firmly and shake it vigorously, and then make some remark about "honest dirt."

One of the most notorious for being immaculate in his appearance was our insurance agent. His pants were always pressed and spotless. He wore a white fedora. His shoes, which I seem to recall were white, looked like he had just purchased them ten minutes ago. His hands were pale, soft, and manicured. His initials were "F.E.," and my brother and I referred to him as "Effie."

One day my dad was working near the front of the barn when "Effie" appeared, resplendent as the lilies of the fields. He always approached his task of selling insurance as a sacred trust, a mission for the world's salvation; and he pursued his victims with intensity and persistence.

My dad shook his hand enthusiastically, leaving a residue on it. Then, as Effie went into his pitch, Dad gradually worked his way down into the bowels of the barn. In order for his message to be heard, Effie had to follow him. So intent was Effie in watching where he stepped, and so distracted by the cobwebs he encountered, and so flustered by the odors that assailed his nostrils, that he forgot his well-rehearsed sales pitch and withdrew in confusion.

The scene must have left quite a dramatic impression on us kids, and I'm sure our presence at the event contributed to our resplendent salesman's confusion because we have frequently related the occasion over the years.

And, of course, I felt you should know about this for your growth and self improvement and carry the knowledge of it to your grave.

A Bee in the Mail Box

By Father Elstan
November 1994

As is my routine, one morning a couple of months ago I walked out to the mail box to retrieve the Minneapolis *Star Tribune* with the intentions of quickly scanning the headlines to determine what vows our legislators had made the previous day -- to cut the deficit, to reduce taxes, to put an end to crime, etc., etc., and blah, blah, blah -- and to get a quick fix on who had killed whom during the night, when my hand caught fire!

I've heard of this happening but never put stock in the reports, where someone suddenly burst into flames, but I was quickly becoming a believer.

Then I noticed the source of the conflagration. There was a bee in the mailbox, reading my paper with his morning cigar. He objected to the interruption and expressed his objection by pumping about three liters of poison into my hand. I brushed him off with a quick gesture and he flopped off, leaving his stinger and a large portion of his intestines behind. I didn't mourn his subsequent demise.

This little beggar of a bee had been a resident of a hive that had been building up in the maple tree outside my window. He should have been busy along with his fellow brothers and sisters, and drones, on the construction of the hive and the housekeeping and whatnot, instead of reading my paper.

Although he -- my attacker -- was sloughing off while the rest of his fellow bees were gainfully employed, he had this in common with them: his rotten attitude.

They -- these belligerent bees -- go about their business with the belief they are the only ones that have a right to function in a certain area. They zip about with a scowl on their faces, making a noise that is angry and threatening -- even when nobody is bothering them.

They seem to interpret every move of their close neighbors as directed against them, and they attack -- even when there's no good reason, and they do so with such zeal that it frequently costs them their own lives.

Their nasty behavior, in this case, resulted in the squirrels and birds, who had been using the big maple as their playground, to abandon the area -- nor have they returned yet, long after the Orkin exterminating company dealt the hive a well deserved blow to its existence.

In all the eons of bees' existence, they have never seemed to learn that in this life, to have pleasant neighbors they must be pleasant themselves; and that in the final analysis we generally get what we give and what we deserve. May they rest in peace.

St. Victoria Church News

from Editor Sue
December 1994

Due to popular demand, Father's classic, "If Maude Had Visited Bethlehem," from the December, 1992, issue of the *Gazette*, is being reprinted here for this Christmas season -- and Father's pen gets a reprieve. Enjoy.

Sunday Football

by Father Elstan
January 1995

It seemed like it was destined to be an idyllic Sunday afternoon. The morning Masses were over; the crowds had dispersed; and the contributions of the faithful had been counted, recorded, and wrapped for the bank. They had been deposited in the bank's handy outdoor container, safe from the grasp of predatory persons; and all that lay before me was to turn on and watch a football game in which I had more than a passing interest.

I settled back in my recliner, flicked on the station, made room for Maude beside me in the seat, and we were just on time for the kickoff.

The wind blew the ball off the tee. The kicker, after taking ten minutes to figure out what happened, replaced the ball. The wind blew it off again. After consulting his teammates, the kicker selected one of them to hold the ball on the tee. During this time the announcer, Joe Theisman, was discovering an omen in all this -- favorable to the receiving team.

Finally the kickoff. There was a long run back, but an illegal block in the process. Another official discovered an infraction on the kicking team. Joe T. began to analyze the whole thing, using a brand of English that would give a professor of our beautiful language the screaming meemies; and, from past experience, I knew it would take some time before play would be resumed so I flicked over to PBS to see a lion creeping through the grass toward a small animal of the deer family.

After what I thought was enough time, I switched back to the game. I was too sanguine. The argument was still in progress, but I waited it out.

Finally the snap. The ball was fumbled and everybody on both teams tried to recover it. The officials began to peel off the players from the pile -- one at a time -- and, again from experience, I knew a considerable time span would be involved in the process.

Back to the lion and the deer, the former still in a stealth mode, the latter eating grass in serene innocence.

Back to the game. After a few meaningless plays, into which Joe T. read much significance, one team called a time-out. That's always a couple of minutes, so back to the Serengeti.

Returning to the game, the other team had called a time-out.

Back to the plains of Africa where the lion had just made his leap and, after watching the chase for some time, I went back to the game, where the first quarter had just come to an end.

On the tropical landscape the pursuit was still in progress. I watched it too long. By the time I got back to the game, two touchdowns had been scored. Joe T. was in a frenzy of excitement, which excitement he expressed inarticulately.

I watched a few plays, during which nothing happened until one of the gladiators was injured. Joe T. diagnosed the injury immediately and assured us all the men would be back for the second half of play.

By the time I got back from Africa the two-minute warning had come up, and the deer had escaped the lion. The big cat was lying in the grass with his tongue hanging out, plotting his next conquest; and the deer was bounding about on the plain looking for his companions from whom he had been separated.

Back for the second half. The score was tied -- I heard just before play resumed. Small wonder, because, according to Joe T., every one of the players on both sides were candidates for the Hall of Fame; and if each one didn't get a berth on the pro bowl team a monumental injustice would be done to both "he and I."

Just when things were heating up, the doorbell rang. By the time I got back to the game, two TD's had been scored -- and a field goal -- and a two-point conversion.

I watched the game progress with nothing happening except the usual time-outs, injuries, penalties, and one fight. Each time it was evident that there would be a length of time before the game would resume, I went back to PBS to watch some nut swimming with sharks. I'd get back to the game in time to hear somebody selling automobiles or cornflakes or something else I couldn't do without.

With two minutes to go, the score was close and the loser was close to scoring -- when the telephone rang. By the time that was over, so was the game. The next day I looked for the score in the sports page. Either I overlooked it or the paper neglected to print it.

Better Schmardt than Vet

by Father Elstan
February 1995

I was up against it for a subject to babble about this month -- and aware of the fertile imagination of our beloved *Gazette* editor, I presented my problem to her. She came across with an entire page of suggestions, one of which was: "What's it like to be Scottish in a land of Germans and Norwegians?" That one reminded me of an incident my father told about on proper and frequent occasions.

He was a skinny kid of nineteen, living on the edge of a neighborhood that was so Catholic it was unaware of the existence of any other religion (My father referred to the enclave as the "Holy Land."), and so German they decorated their buildings with sauerkraut. The word "clannish" springs to mind when this group is mentioned.

One of the major-domos of this exclusive group had a large building of some description on his property that he wanted to move to another location. The project called for a large number of advisers, observers, and a few to do some work. My grandfather sent the old dad up to the scene of action; his role was work -- as called for by "da boss."

The group at the site of the excitement conversed in German with each other -- and with the attitude that anyone unable to understand German was some sort of inferior species. They only spoke English -- and rather bad English -- when they issued an order to my dad. He felt isolated.

One final step before the building could proceed on its journey to its new location called for someone to crawl under the jacked-up building and remove a spike, or wedge, or something. None of the "inner circle" could fit in the space where the task had to be carried out, having spent too much time in close contact with too much mashed potatoes, beer, and bratwurst. They were totally dependent on my dad to accomplish the task.

"Ya, Donald, you crawl unter dere und yank oudt dat schpike," or "dat vedge," or vatever.

About the time he had wiggled his way to the spot where he had to be for the job, it started to rain. Excited voices from without urged him on to get the job done and get it done quickly.

"Mach schnell, Kid! Ve are getting vet!"

My father told them it was dry where he was. They suggested he shouldn't "get schmardt!"

As the rain increased in volume, the voices from without faded and died. My father curled up and went to sleep. By the time he woke up the sun was out and the crowd had gone home. He never did remove the "schpike" or "vedge" or vatever. He went home -- and wondered ever since how they ever got the job done. He never went back to find out.

The Wily Scot

by Father Elstan
March 1995

One more incident from the life and times of "The Wily Scot" -- my dad.

You may recall I regaled you last month with the incident in his youth when he held up the entire operation of a building-moving project in the neighborhood adjoining ours -- a neighborhood that was populated by a very turned-in and exclusionary citizenry. That was the neighborhood my father referred to as the "Holy Land."

When I was preschool age, a sensation was created when a family -- roughly paralleling our own in number of kids, size of farm, age of parents, religion, politics, etc. -- moved in on the border of "our neighborhood" and "theirs" -- "theirs" being sacred and unbreachable territory.

The father of this family didn't qualify for membership in the Holy Land, mainly on the grounds that he was a recent arrival, but also because he didn't sport a stomach that looked like the store room of a brewery; and he didn't have jowls and a face that looked like an inflamed liver.

In a short time his family and ours played, worked, and worshipped together.

To present an example of how close we were, twice a year the old folks -- our parents -- went to confession; and before the big ordeal came around they would gather together in a semi-serious confab to help examine each other's consciences.

Also, once a year generally, in the fall if I remember correctly, the unofficial end of the fiscal year, the two dads would sit down one evening under our big maple tree in the yard and go over the past year's work and determine who had helped whom, and how often, and arrive at an amicable financial agreement.

There was nothing on paper -- just the combined memories of the two parties. On this one occasion, after all was said and done, it came out my dad owed him $10 for the year's exchanges. That settled, they sat around and told wild stories for about an hour and a half; and the neighbor got up, stretched, and headed for his old Model-T to go home to his wife and children and an honest man's rest.

He was in the car, the motor was running, and the conversation was still in progress. He finally said, "Yeah, well, I'd better get along or Mama will think I am off with another woman, ha, ha."

Dad said, "Yeah, I'll see you in church. And as for that $10, you can pay me any time it's convenient."

He answered, "Okay. I'll get it to you as soon as I can." And he drove off.

I don't know how far up the road he was before he realized he was the one who was owed the tenner, but when he did, he forgot what "Mama" might think about his being gone so long, turned around, and came right back. My father had the ten dollars waiting for him when he drove into the yard.

My Sister the Elder Statesman

by Father Elstan
April 1995

My oldest sister Blanche died last month. She was also the oldest of the eight of us. And she exploited her exalted position as the elder statesman shamelessly.

From the beginning she assumed the role of protector of our safety from the forces of evil that surrounded us lesser members of the family -- an attitude that was a constant source of embarrassment, especially to my brother and me who didn't see the need of that kind of attention.

She also let it be known that her advanced accomplishments in the field of academia put her in the position of being our professor. In fact, I remember the teacher telling my folks on one occasion to have her ease off in this department lest we be taught material way ahead of our age and not sufficiently master the lessons designed for our own level. That was a happy day for us peons.

She was always disgustingly zealous in setting the table, washing the dishes, dusting the furniture, and mopping the floor -- habits that cast the rest of us kids in a rather dim light. I have a picture of her swatting my brother and me across the behinds with a wet mop when we walked on "her" kitchen floor with dirty boots just after it had been scrubbed -- mainly by Mom, but with her invaluable assistance.

In those days of our grade schooling, it was practically a given that the girl who graduated with the best grades -- and it was just taken for granted that that would be a girl -- went to Good Counsel Academy as a postulant in the Order of Notre Dame Sisters.

In Blanche's grade there was that anomaly of a boy who had excellent marks. It was always nip and tuck between Jerome Eischens and Blanche as to who would have the better grades. At graduation it was announced that Blanche had nosed him out by a fraction of a point, but there always lingered a suspicion that the thing was rigged. The Sisters couldn't realize a vocation from Jerome. He couldn't pass the physical. Let is be noted that he was a gentleman about it, and big spirited, and the two were good friends all through their lives.

After two years in the convent -- and, I suspect, when she realized she couldn't start out as a Mother Superior -- Blanche came home and followed the vocation she had been preparing for all her life: bossing kids around -- her own now, seven in all -- protecting them, and teaching them.

A device she used in rearing them was to be vocal in her attacks on the evils in the world -- politics, society, and individuals -- like a minor prophet of the Old Testament berating the sinners of the cities of the plains.

She, as it were, created in her own family a peer group from which her kids didn't dare to stray. And none of them ever did.

If there are any deficiencies among the angels and saints, I'm sure they've heard about it now. And if they needed it -- and have behinds -- they have felt the application of her wet mop judiciously applied at the proper time.

St. Victoria Church News

from Editor Sue
May 1995

To fans of Father Elstan, the popular purveyor of piety and pleasantries at the St. Victoria Catholic Church, hang in there till next month. He ran out of ink in April -- but his candle still flickers.

The Flock and Floodgate

by Father Elstan
June 1995

Peering into the future I find myself anticipating retirement with considerable excitement. For one thing, I am congenitally indolent.

But also I have always wanted to put on permanent written record (I don't know what other kind of "permanent record" there may be) gripes, complaints, irritations, and frustrations that are peculiarly clerical in nature -- or, more specifically, pastoral.

Some of these complaints are general in nature; some are my own private property. But I can't do that now while I'm still pastoring a flock without the possibility of grave repercussions.

However, there is one that is quite a universal irritation to pastors, and that can probably be discussed without danger of a large segment of the congregation dropping out of the church -- besides which those who create the irritation are not of the type that are given to reading classical literature, and so will probably never be aware of this composition anyway.

I have reference to those who leave church before the Mass, or service, is over. It is a disturbing condition that is frequently discussed in clerical circles.

Some creative ways to correct the problem have surfaced in these discussions. One pastor made an announcement -- in the middle of the service so that those who were guilty would hear it -- that "from now on those men who have kidney trouble and those women who are over forty are asked to leave the church first when the worship is concluded." He had considerable success with that approach.

Some radical ideas are to have the ushers lock the doors toward the end of the liturgy, but the local fire departments take a dim view of that solution.

One even suggested, in an angry reaction, that he intended to station a group of men outside the church with assault weapons. Even the NRA frowned at that solution, and I suspect the Pope would have frowned equally as severely had the procedure reached his papal ears.

A suggestion has surfaced on occasion that each Sunday we have a drawing, at which the winner must be present to collect. Somehow or other this method has never acquired the status of universal acceptance.

I thought of putting forth the idea of saying a prayer during the worship that God would cause all those who leave early to trip and fall down as they rush out. Someone of a more spiritual nature would counter that it would be better to say the prayer *for* the delinquents.

One local pastor is doing something that works. He has what he calls "the joke of the week." He tells this joke right after the Mass concludes. Everyone stays to hear it. My concern is: How long will it take before he has to start repeating himself? He could possibly ask for a transfer after he runs out of gags and start afresh elsewhere.

Most pastors settle for just seething and growling about it all when in the company of his fellow pastors, and take some consolation from Sacred Scripture where it is noted that when it comes to entering the kingdom of heaven the last (to leave the church) shall be first, and the first shall be last.

Why are Back Pews Attractive?

by Father Elstan
July 1995

Having in last month's piece unleashed a salvo at those who dash out the church door sometime before the service is ended and it not having resulted in a protest march by those who were addressed by the salvo, I feel emboldened to remark about another group whose behavior results in wrinkled brows and concerned headshaking among pastors of flocks.

Parenthetically, the discussion about those who get off the mark before the gun goes off at the end of services hasn't resulted in those changing their behavior -- as far as I can observe.

Nor do I expect noticeable results in the class I confront now. As a matter of fact, the group that storms the backdoor exit like a buffalo stampede prior to the end of services is, to a large extent, the same as make it a point to attend church as far from the front as possible.

It is an interesting question and study. What is it about the back of the church that is so attractive or, to put it another way, what is so repulsive about the pews in the front of the church? What is it that prompts someone who comes to church to be as remote from the action in church as possible?

As I've been confronted with these questions, some interesting answers have surfaced. "I have arthritis in my knees and it's hard to walk that far." Then, at communion time they will walk that far -- and all the way back.

"I feel embarrassed walking in the aisle past all those people." Yes, what a disgrace to be seen going to church.

"I can't get out of church after it's over as quickly as I would like." That answer usually leaves the inquisitor a bit speechless.

The tendency under discussion expresses itself in such extremes as causing the short benches in the back of the church reserved for the ushers to be the first ones filled, which the ushers tolerate in a spirit of Christian meekness.

It also results in the choir loft being filled up quickly -- about as far from the altar as it is possible to get without falling out of the rose window. I hesitate to be too critical of those who crowd up there. I used to do that myself when I was in grade school, and the motive was to get as far removed from the all-seeing eye of Sister Mary Marcella as possible. She had a left jab that rivaled that of Joe Louis. Besides, it was comforting to note I wasn't the worst kid present. Elmer was always there curled up in a bench and sound asleep.

Come to think of it, I hesitate to criticize any who choose the back benches. With my luck, as soon as I would make a public issue of it, the Gospel for the Mass would certainly be the parable of the Pharisee who strode up to the front of the synagogue as far as he could go and told God what a fine chap he was -- and the humble publican, who didn't think he was worthy to be in the front bench, so he stayed as far back as he could get and pointed out what a washout he was. His prayer was heard rather than the other's.

Confronted with this irrefutable logic, what could I say?

Shut Off the Lights!

by Father Elstan
August 1995

Since I am on the subject of "pastoral gripes," there is one that can not go untreated. I refer to the almost universal custom of the public to leave a building with lights on, thermostats wide open, and doors unlocked and ajar.

For a pastor who is always conscious of the upcoming monthly utility bill, this kind of irresponsible neglect tends to distract and render his meditations more materialistic than spiritual and his prayer life virtually null and void.

With regard to lights, there is any number of pious souls who linger on in church after Mass to immerse themselves in profound contemplation -- and leave in a state of semi-ecstasy totally unconscious of the existence of the light switch.

Especially vulnerable to the unconcern of a thoughtless public is the light switch in the bathroom. Parenthetically, what is the biological principle that goes to work on a set of kidneys the minute they come within a block of a church?

Questions present themselves to the conscientious pastor, such as: Would these miscreants be as negligent in their own homes? Would they be more alert if a curse, commensurate to their crime, would take effect each time they failed? Would they listen if a ghostly voice were to be automatically activated each time the last one left the building? -- "Did you turn off the lights? Is the thermostat shut off? Did you lock the door?"

These are possibilities that can occupy our dreams on occasion.

There is just one circumstance that is more agitating than those described above. That is when we find ourselves guilty of the same sin of omission, committed because of our preoccupation with the laxity of members of our flock.

Not long ago I looked out into the church and noticed the two lights in the back still on, and no one using them. I charged back, slammed off the one switch, and noticed the next morning I had overlooked the second switch.

Recently I noticed a light on in the Parish Center, just before I was going to retire. I faced the perils of the night and inclement weather to journey across the parking lot to correct the problem. I unlocked the door, went in and turned off the lights, checked out the thermostat, and came back to the house thinking dark and unkind thoughts. The next day I noticed I had left the door unlocked.

The combination of these two circumstances -- the public's gross negligence and our own easily explained and readily forgiven slip-ups -- may help you to understand why, now and then, you will notice a pastor wandering aimlessly around the yard, talking to himself, sticking straws in his hair and carrots in his ears, and thumbing frantically through the yellow pages under the headings of "support groups" and/or "psychiatrists."

Corrugated Clerical Brows

by Father Elstan
September 1995

When I think of retiring, a degree of trepidation creeps in on me. What will I do with all the extra time? Will I begin to deteriorate more quickly? Will I feel useless?

But then it occurs to me, "I will no longer have to have any more weddings," and suddenly the prospect of retiring becomes enormously attractive.

The hassles connected to nuptials can best be exemplified by, and in the person of, the "wedding coordinator." She -- it is always a "she" -- has

184

corrugated more clerical brows and grayed more pastoral hairs than anyone with whom he came into contact on a regular basis.

The wedding coordinator was a standard feature in Memphis when I was stationed there some time ago. She was hired at an exorbitant fee and was something of a status symbol. Any wedding that was going to be written up in the daily paper had to have a wedding coordinator.

She was usually a female of generous proportions who portrayed a consciousness of the staggering responsibilities of her office. There was always a pair of glasses draped around her neck on a conspicuously flashy string of some sort, which rested on her massive bosom, and was placed on her nose and removed from it at proper intervals.

In her right hand was a jeweled pen and in the crook of her left arm reposed a clipboard with about forty-seven pages of memos. She was always in a nervous dither because she had to boss the whole procedure without appearing to be bossy. That made her consultations with the clergyman especially tense.

"Now, when the procession up the middle aisle begins, should the girls lead with their left foot or their right foot? Is there any directive in the church on this question?"

"Yes, the Council of Baltimore specifically stated they are to lead with their left foot."

Wedding Coordinator: "Does the church have any objection to the girls taking a step -- and pausing for a moment before taking the next step during the procession?"

Clergyman: "The Council of Trent discourages this practice but doesn't place an excommunication on it."

WC: "Can we take a moment to determine when the church wants the wedding party to sit, kneel, and stand?"

Clergyman: "The diocesan directives are not real specific on this subject except to say they may not stand on their heads during the ceremony."

She checks that memo on her clipboard sheets and about this time a half a dozen members of the wedding party come in late and she reviews with them the progress made so far and consults her clipboard memos as they spend a quarter of an hour introducing themselves all around.

The long night wears on. One item after the other on her all-important clipboard is checked off with a flourish. All items are reviewed and half of them are changed.

The practice journey up the aisle is gone through several times, to make sure all start out on their left foot, that all start and stop at the correct time, that the little kids in the party are thoroughly instructed, that the organist and vocalist have their cues down precisely, that all possible contingencies have been discussed and backup plans are in place (What if someone should faint? What if someone fails to show up? Who will pick up the Coca Cola and 7-Up cans from the window sills, benches and floors? Where shall the flowers be placed? Etc. Etc.).

And two hours after the practice has started -- and it started a half hour late -- most of the forty-seven memos have been checked and double checked, and the wedding coordinator has managed to introduce total confusion into the proceedings, the party begins to drift away one at a time, prepared to leave the whole production up to Divine Providence.

When I retire I intend to observe a few wedding practices from a distance to see how far the clergyman who has the wedding has progressed on the road to perfection -- at least in the department of patience.

Baffled by a Blizzard in the Kitchen

by Father Elstan
October 1995

I have had occasion in the past to allude to my deficiency in talent in matters mechanical.

You may recall the time the blush of embarrassment suffused my features when I was driving a 1962 Volkswagen and the motor stalled. In an effort to ascertain the cause I peered under the hood, expecting to see the motor. Those of you who have advanced knowledge of cars and their unique designs will recall that the motor of a 1962 Volkswagen was located in the trunk -- not under the hood.

What kind of a person would locate the motor there instead of where it belongs remains one of the mysteries of the ages. It can only be the result of a warped sense of humor.

This time an unfortunate incident with my refrigerator led to a further revelation of my lack of understanding the inventions of our modern age.

It all came about when I slammed the door on the top part (referred to by those in the know as "the freezer compartment"), and it apparently did not close completely. The next time I looked into the compartment I noticed a considerable buildup of ice.

Applying my unerring sense of logic, I concluded the best way to melt the ice was to leave the door wide open and let in the warm air from the outside to effect the necessary meltdown. To hasten the result, I put a bowl of hot water in the compartment -- and retired, reminding myself to expect a loud bump in the night when the process would loosen the ice on the roof and sides of the box, and so not to be alarmed when it came.

It never came.

The next morning I peeked into the freezer area to be confronted by a glacier. The hot water had frozen; the ice trays and a half consumed box of ice cream, and a number of frozen waffles were locked in the cold grasp of a solid mass.

I mentioned these details to a select group of people who I thought would be sympathetic, and equally as baffled as I was; but I found myself trying to interpret their reactions. There were sly smiles and eyes cast skyward -- and a few pointed questions like: "Did you unplug the refrigerator?"

When it became apparent that I had made some very fundamental errors in my procedure, I expected the details of my mistakes would remain in the group, but it was not to be. The next day when I stopped in at the post office I was subjected to a series of impertinent questions -- and when a bit of knowledge is picked up at the post office, it is equivalent to blazing a headline across Main Street in flashing lights.

It is well for us to learn from others' mistakes, which, of course, is the whole point of this gripping narrative. So if you ever have the problem mentioned above, consult me. I now have all the answers. Or mention it to the right person, who, when she gets her laughter under control, will come and clean out the ice and restore the freezer to functioning in the manner for which it was designed in the first place.

A Buzzing in My Head

by Father Elstan
November 1995

So there I was, minding my own business, standing outside of the house one evening under the porch light; and winged creatures were flitting around the light like a bunch of crazies, having no apparent destination and no evident reason for their flitting, when a moth, who was a member of the kookie crew, was distracted in his flight -- possibly he glanced over his shoulder to see who was passing him on the wrong side -- and he flew straight into my left ear. Well! That will get your attention.

All attempts to dislodge the little bugger resulted in his burrowing ever more deeply into the recesses of my head. One of those attempts involved two members of our group, one of whom stood on my left side and one on my right, blowing into the ear closest to them. This agitated the moth but didn't eject him.

He simply flapped his wings more vigorously as my hair stood on end and my eyes bulged out.

Finally, a member of our crew loaded me into her car and we drove to the emergency room in Waconia. Our friend, the moth, continued to attempt to fly, creating the sensation of a hummingbird flitting around in the depths of my head.

Having arrived at our destination, I was subjected to an inquisition: "Are you allergic to anything?" "Have you ever been treated here before?" "When is your birthday?" "Whom shall we inform in case of an emergency?" Etc., Etc., Etc.

And finally: "What seems to be your trouble?" I wanted to answer to that, "I have this strange buzzing in my head" -- but let it go. I was told to "wait in this room and someone will be along shortly to see you."

The moth and I could both have starved to death before someone did show up -- a nurse with a flashlight. She peered into my ear with her light, saying that sometimes a light will lure a bug out, as if this kind of emergency were routine. Not this bug. He was so deep in he couldn't see the light.

Again I was told to wait, and the doctor would be in "in a minute." I learned a new definition of the word "minute," but, by and by, he sauntered in.

After considerable probing, he took in his hand an instrument that looked like a tenpenny spike. When he began to explore the depths of my head with it, it felt like a tenpenny spike that had been heated to the melting point.

When I informed him in graphic language, accompanied by groans and screams, that it hurt, he casually remarked that that was one of the most sensitive areas of the human body. That bit of information was hardly necessary. I had already arrived at that conclusion all by myself.

Eventually, he removed the moth -- a hardy little beast who was still alive. The doc put it in a plastic envelope and gave it to me and sent me home.

When I got home I threw the moth in the container on my desk and retired, determined to deal harshly with it in the morning. Came the dawn and the envelope was still there, but the moth was gone. My sole consolation is that he may have been as uncomfortable throughout the ordeal as I was.

Dear Aunt Martha

I have noted over the years the persecution to which you have been subjected at our local post office. I have read avidly the column in the *Gazette* that generally features you being badgered by our resident civil servant -- who insists on your having the exact amount of postage on your mail, as if a loyal customer like you could not be cut some slack in these minor matters.

It isn't as if the federal government would go into receivership if you didn't put 83¢ on a bit of mail instead of 82¢, or as if the entire postal system in the country would collapse in confusion if you wrapped a package with a two-inch tape instead of two-and-a-quarter inch.

And I think we could reasonably expect that one who brings so much custom to the post office could anticipate a certain amount of cooperation when she asks for a particular kind of stamp. It just seems right.

It may be of some consolation, my dear Aunt Martha, to know you do not suffer alone. I have been subjected to various indignities at that same location and I can honestly say, "I feel your pain."

For example, when, on rare occasions the post office in a burst of generosity has a cookie and coffee day, and I take advantage of the opportunity to get something back from the business to which I have given so much, I am accused of stuffing extra cookies into my pockets to feed Maude. I tell you, Martha, that hurts.

And how would you like it if, when you walked into the establishment, you were greeted with the words: "Well! Here's Victoria's expert on sin!" -- and other customers give you a quizzical look and back out the door in great haste?

And does your pal, Postmaster Al, put your mail up against the door of your box in such a way that when you open the thing all the pieces fall on the floor?

Well, Aunt Martha, we've been the victims of some severe persecutions, but we bore it all with equanimity and steadfastly; and we are better, nobler people for it. I expect, since Al is retiring now -- and one is seriously tempted to ask, "Retire from what?" -- our spiritual life will deteriorate, since our former source of suffering will be gone; our patience and humility will no longer be tested; and we will be apt to become complacent.

But we'll miss the old grouch, won't we, Martha? When we go down to the post office and throw something at him -- like a barb, for instance, and he isn't there -- well, we'll miss him.

Sincerely,
Father Elstan Coghill, OFM
December 1995

The Friar with the "Cadazy" Accent

by Father Elstan
January 1996

You may remember that, some time back, I took it upon myself to introduce you to some of the characters with whom I intermingled as a Franciscan friar. It occurred to me that the list was incomplete without the name of Father Aloysius Fromm, the rector of the minor seminary when I attended it -- four years of high school and two years of college.

In private conversation -- out of earshot from him -- we referred to him by one of his nicknames: "Alley" – as if he were some sort of narrow passage between two rows of buildings, or "Alloys" – as if he were some kind of chemical compound, or "Cueball" -- which was the most accurate name since his head and a cueball sported about the same amount of hair.

Fr. A. (take your choice) reflected a massive dignity. In his large and hairless head were two eyes that always seemed to be partially closed. He had a complexion like an inflamed liver (Have I used that analogy before?) and a body that could have been the inspiration for Shakespeare's classical Friar Tuck.

Although he was well educated, he still retained a degree of an accent from his background, which, of course, was German. He always wore an expression that gave the impression he was harboring a secret sorrow. It also gave the impression that he was fully cognizant of many infractions of rules and regulations.

The combination of all these qualities amounted to his being the ideal rector of the seminary. His very presence in the building tended to enforce discipline.

Each September when we returned from vacation, "Cueball" would be standing at the front of the building to "welcome" us back -- sometimes with a remark of surprise that we were back at all, based on our previous year's performance.

The first order of business after our return was a speech to the subdued seminarians by the powerful orator. We all assembled in the study hall and, after a sufficient delay, he walked in and down the aisle -- like a one-man procession -- to his desk on an elevated platform, from whence he looked out over the quivering student body with a stern and slightly sad expression on his beefy face.

Finally he coughed and started by first wagging his head in a meaningful manner. Then the predictable first words: "Quo vadis!" His German accent came through in his Latin. The "Quo" was pronounced "Ka-Voh," and the "a" in "vadis" sounded like the "a" in "bad" or "mad," which gave the phrase more weight.

After getting off the mark with "Quo vadis," he treated us to the most dramatic pause ever employed in oratory. During the pause, everybody present -- under their breath -- continued with the translation: "Wither goest thou."

All of us who had been there any length of time knew the entire speech by heart. It was always word for word the same, and we had heard it twice a year -- at the beginning of each school term in September and the resumption of school after the Christmas break. The seminary mimics had a field day with the speech for the first few weeks afterwards, and there was no shortage of them.

It is hard to imagine that one who gave the impression he was absorbed with only weighty and serious matters could have any interest in something so mundane as baseball, but Cueball had an ardent passion for the old Milwaukee Braves.

I can't imagine why he did this, but when Fr. Bernardine and I were stationed together at Guardian Angels during the '50's, "Alley," if that's what you prefer, would come to Chaska and spend his vacation with us -- who had given him more grief during our seminary years than most.

This one year the Braves were in a close race for the pennant, and each evening the three of us would sit around the radio to listen to the game, and thrill to the exploits of Lou Burdette, Johnny Sain, and Warren Spahn.

One evening it was very stormy and the reception was so bad we were missing most of the broadcast, and it was a crucial game. Fr. B. and I decided to get in the car and drive up to the cemetery -- a very high spot in the area.

We were getting into the front seat when we looked around -- and there was Alloys. It was a big surprise, because at that time of his life he wasn't so mobile any more, and he had always been of regular habit, and usually retired before a game was finished.

As he composed himself in the back seat, he said, "If you can be crazy (pronounce "ca-dazy"), I can be 'cadazy' too."

As we drove up to the cemetery he said, in his most formal manner -- everything he said was in a formal manner -- "Let us see vot Hendedy can do tonight." A great slugger with the Braves in those years was Henry Aaron, which, of course, he pronounced, "Hendedy Addon."

Alley, if we had only known when we were mere students and you were the almighty rector that you were capable of being as "cadazy" as the next guy, we would have been spared a lot of anxiety and stress during our years of study, you son of a gun.

We Kissed the Ground

by Father Elstan
February 1996

Say -- did I ever tell you about the time I came close to winding up on the bottom of Lake Superior? It was when I was stationed in St. Paul with Fr. Hugolinus.

Occasionally we would jump into the car early in the A.M. and drive up to Bayfield, Wisconsin, to visit our friend, Fr. Regis. After the events I am about to relate to you, however, the word "friend" is used in its broadest possible connotation.

It was a Monday in March. We arranged to take Fr. Kay, a neighboring pastor in St. Paul, along on our adventure. Bayfield, in March, doesn't have a lot to offer for diversion. After having reviewed the weather, which we unanimously agreed had been quite warm for that time of the year; solved some of the problems the elected officials in Washington had failed to solve; and discussed the progress of the church, we were about to descend to the level of playing Chinese checkers -- when Fr. Regis said, "I've got a few parishioners on Madeline Island whom I haven't seen all winter. Let's drive over and visit them."

Madeline Island is a few miles out in the lake from Bayfield. It sounded good to us. We piled into his big station wagon and struck out across the ice. We noticed the water coming up around the wheels, and a peculiar wavey sensation as we drove along. But we figured Regis for a prudent man who knew the territory, and thought little of it.

When we arrived at the folks whom we had come to visit, they looked like they were seeing ghosts. Without preamble they asked, "How did you g-get over here?"

In what I felt was a rather offhanded manner, Fr. Regis said, "We drove over."

They said, "B-but there hasn't been a car out on that ice for two weeks! How are you going to get back?"

Regis again had the ready answer. "We'll drive back."

It might be well here to point out that my three companions totaled in weight about a half a ton. They had all done themselves proud among the starches and carbohydrates -- and it showed. And the station wagon weighed about as much as a boxcar -- fully loaded.

We started back -- with the doors wide open, and we were all crouched to spring. We were more aware of the water rising around the wheels and the "give" in the ice than we were on the way over. Some of – no, all of the confidence we had in Fr. R.'s judgment had entirely dissipated.

Safe on shore at last, we kissed the ground and then held an informal competition to see who could come up with the most descriptive names for Fr. R.

Fr. Hugolinus said that all the way back from the island he was imagining the headlines in the next day's *Bayfield Tribune* -- or *Gazette*, or whatever it is: "Local Pastor Disappears!" "Car Missing!" "Foul Play Suspected!" Etc. etc.

Well, old Regis came close to being the victim of foul play by us. And, of all things, we thought of the best names for him when we were on the road back to St. Paul that night. Isn't that always the way it is? Your juiciest lines occur to you when it's too late.

God Intervened
Through the Tail of a Cow

by Father Elstan
March 1996

I wonder if there is not a number of clergy in the vast reading audience of *The Victoria Gazette* who have been asked, possibly often, to tell the story of their call to follow the life of a minister of the Gospel.

I have been quizzed on numerous occasions and, when I am, I have to dig the old toe into the dirt and do an imitation of a kid who is being asked by a stern and frightful teacher why his homework is missing.

I hear the story of others who have responded to a vocation to the ministry, and they all seem to have had some kind of spiritual experience or sign from God that directed them to the seminary -- and in my case it was the tail of a cow that started me thinking. No private revelation or direct communication from above had anything to do with it.

It was the hot summer of 1934. It fell to my lot in the evening to try to coax some milk out of this cow. She had been lying down with her tail in the gutter. The flies were having their evening repast off of her. The temperature was in the three-figure range. She switched at flies incessantly but made more contact with me than with the flies.

By the time I finished the job I was fly-bitten, frustrated, and full of fertilizer; and it occurred to me that there had to be a better way of going through life than under a dumb and dirty cow.

About the same time I noted that the priests in our parish never had to milk cows -- nor harness horses nor hoe weeds nor do any kind of manual labor that revolted me so much; and they still seemed to get a good deal of respect and good press from everybody; and I thought ... hmmmm!

The fall after the encounter with the cow, my oldest sister left for Good Counsel Academy in Mankato, presumably to be a nun. That got her a good deal of recognition, and it seemed to me she was launching out on an adventure that was equivalent to Columbus' discoveries and explorations.

Mankato was so far away it was in a different county, and you had to take a train to get there -- and what could be more exciting than that! All that, along with my constant effort to upstage my sister, I again thought ... hmmmm!

I neglected to tell anybody about my decision -- thinking nobody would believe me anyway, and some would double up in uncontrollable laughter. I had no idea the amount of preparation that was called for, but finally I had to let my mom know, and the last two weeks of the summer of '36 were a whirlwind of activity.

Shortly before I left home -- to go practically halfway around the world -- to Chicago! -- my dad said that whatever I did I had to stay at least two weeks no matter how homesick I got because he had a half-dollar bet with my grandmother that I would stay two weeks.

My grandmother had good reason to anticipate a short stay at the seminary -- based on her observations of my tendency to criminal behavior, my less than wholesome language, and her low opinion of boys of my age group in general.

She figured the seminary staff would usher me out the backdoor within a day or two of my arrival. I determined to double-cross her at all costs. I even got my dad to promise I would collect half of the half-dollar if I saw to it that he won the bet.

By the time I was in the seminary for two weeks I was completely contented, and never considered the possibility of quitting -- but I'm sure the seminary officials considered the possibility of handing me a one-way ticket on numerous occasions; and somehow it all worked out without any visions or revelations or getting knocked off a horse by a bolt of lightning or divine intervention -- or wasn't there?

Mrs. Wren Visited Grandma

by Father Elstan
April 1996

Not long ago a group of us were gathered in discussion, and one or the other offered incontrovertible evidence garnered from a keen sense of observation, that "spring" -- employing a well-turned phrase -- "was just around the corner."

To substantiate their claim they presented the argument that birds of various sizes and colors were being sighted -- birds whose absence over the previous many months had been apparent. Some of the more astute members of the discussion directed our attention to the change in the weather to give credence to their claim that spring was here or about to arrive. I preferred to simply look at the calendar.

All this give and take recalled to mind the return of a family of wrens to our yard when I and my siblings were mere rambunctious kids.

One winter day my father brought an armful of tools into the kitchen, and some small timbers, rolled the oilcloth off the table and unfurled a drawing -- a drawing of a log cabin house. After hours of sawing, whittling, nailing, and gluing, he produced a sturdy, rustic, wren house.

When it was just the right time, he secured it to the top of an eight-foot pole in the yard, an anchor for one end of the clothes line. The other end was attached to a black walnut tree, under which my grandma sat and crocheted through the warm afternoons.

A jenny wren happened by, and when she saw the log cabin house she slammed on the brakes, circled the house, and eventually landed on it. After checking out the foundation, the roof, and the timbers, she got around to the door -- just large enough for her and too small for "those stinking sparrows." She ducked inside and shortly peered out with a smile on her face. Everything was satisfactory.

She chose for her decorating scheme soft gray material, and spotted it on Grandma's head. As Grandma, sitting as rigid as a statue, worked her magic with her needles, she began to talk and chirp softly to Mrs. Wren.

Gradually the little beggar worked her way down the clothesline toward Grandma, keeping a wary watch out for sharp-eyed chicken hawks, predatory cats, and wild kids.

Eventually she cautiously hopped up on Grandma's shoulder, chose just the right strand of gray hair, pulled it out of Grandma's head and returned to her log cabin retreat with her prize. This process was repeated again and again that afternoon and for several days thereafter, until the bird's home was satisfactorily decorated, padded, and prepared for a family.

We kids watched the whole procedure with awe and fascination, and in total silence. Mom had given us an order -- and we knew she meant it because she used our first and second names in giving the order that we were not to make a sound nor sudden move and scare the wren away. It was made clear that anything in the nature of a disturbance on our part would result in terrible -- although vague -- consequences.

The wren, or her offspring, returned year after year and the whole scene was repeated -- until Grandma died. It got to be a rite of spring, our favorite sign of the season.

"Little John," the Irish Behemoth

by Father Elstan
May 1996

Earlier this month Fr. John McManamon died. We started out together in the seminary in 1936. Even then, at the age of 14, he was larger and stronger than most grown men; and he continued to grow larger and stronger -- and more awkward -- as the years went on. And he seemed to be oblivious of his prodigious power.

He was considered by some to be a bit slow because he had a peculiar form of dyslexia; but he was, in fact, pretty sharp. He would read a sentence and substitute synonyms for the written word that had no similarity in sound or lettering. If the sentence read, for example, "We drove our car up to the bank of the river," Jack might read, "We pulled our automobile up to the edge of the stream." It was great sport trying to follow him when he had to read publicly.

Shortly after ordination he went down to Brazil to beat Christianity into the heads of the poor natives. They immediately dubbed him, "Little John." It was in the mission field that some of the more remarkable stories about him emerged.

A lot of his work called for travel with an outboard motor on the Tapajos River. "Little John" would pull up on the shore, detach the motor, and when the villagers came down to greet him he waved to them -- with the motor. No doubt that disposed them to listen more intently to his instructions.

On one occasion he had to visit a community deep in the jungle. For transportation he had a horse. Some distance from the village the horse collapsed. Carrying Jack's 290 pounds I can sympathize with the horse. I could sympathize if it had been an elephant. Granted that the Brazilian version of a horse is condensed, it was still an impressive sight to the natives to see him stride into their village with the horse slung over his shoulder.

He came to a village one time and his flock had reserved a hut for him in which they installed a hammock. At the end of his long day, he collapsed into his sleeping arrangement and pulled the entire house in on himself.

In Brazil it is customary for men, when they haven't seen each other for a long time, to greet with a huge hug. Bishop Ryan stopped at Jack's place one time and, in keeping with the custom of the country, embraced enthusiastically -- too enthusiastically on Little John's part. He broke three of the bishop's ribs.

I know how the bishop felt. On one occasion when we were in the major seminary, our class was sent on a work detail in an old '38 flatbed truck. I was sitting on the floor and "Johnny Mac" was standing up surveying the passing scene. Suddenly the truck lurched and he crashed down on my rib cage.

They scraped me off the floor and took me to the hospital with three (he seemed to specialize in "three's") broken ribs. I was confined to my room for a couple of weeks. Every day old Mac, looking like a whipped dog, came to see me and inquired about my health.

I spent my long hours of recuperation thinking of rotten things to say to him the next time he showed up, trying to keep it within the boundaries of religious decorum: "You big fat, clumsy Mick!!" and "If I should croak I'm coming back to haunt you!" and "The next time we're out on that truck I hope you fall out on the pavement and land on your fat head! Not that it would hurt you any! There's enough bone up there to protect you from any blow!"

He took it all with humility and came back every day for more. I don't know who was more repentant after it was all over -- he or I.

At any rate, he won't be crushing bishops' and classmates' ribs and wearing out horses and knocking down houses any more, but will probably be spending half of his eternity apologizing to St. Peter for accidentally tearing the pearly gates off their hinges -- the big, fat, dumb, Irish behemoth!

Looking Ahead

by Father Elstan
June 1996

I have been subjected to some pressure by a certain party to use this column to say "farewell," since I will be departing from Victoria in July. But there is a danger in acceding to that request of sinking into a morass of saccharine sentimentality, and we must forestall that unhappy event at all costs, must we not?

It is in order, I believe, however, to point out that with my departure an era of over a century of service to the St. Victoria parish by the Franciscans of the Sacred Heart Province comes to an end. These men implanted a spirit in this worshipping community that is unique and quite exemplary, I believe.

Parenthetically, Father Bernardine Hahn and I will be the only living ex-pastors of the parish -- assuming that neither one of us hands in our dinner pail before about the Fourth of July.

Looking ahead -- the new pastor at St. Victoria will be Father Robert White, a young, vigorous, dedicated, and congenial man who will serve you all joyfully and conscientiously, I am convinced.

Continuing to look ahead -- I will be going to a place in Michigan which is close to the Mackinac Bridge and Mackinac Island. It is a parish slightly smaller than St. Victoria but with a significant appendage: a shrine called, "The Cross in the Woods."

The town is Indian River. The parish and the shrine operate independently of each other but are administered by the same personnel -- Father Donard, a classmate of mine from the seminary, and the head honcho, and Father Flavius, one year ahead of us in the seminary and the first one I met when I landed on the seminary grounds in 1936.

Fr. Flavius took it upon himself to show me the best spots to hide for smoking a cigarette, against which there was some sort of ridiculous prohibition, and the safest place to sneak out of bounds -- and imparted other bits of valuable information without which a chap couldn't function properly at the school. He had already been there a year when I came and so was privy to a vast store of helpful hints and useful cautions.

With regard to the shrine, "The Cross in the Woods," a brief history might be in order. Back in the '40's the bishop of Grand Rapids noted that there was no Catholic Church in Indian River nor any place reasonably close. He ran his finger down the list of his personnel and stopped when he came to the name of Monsignor Brophy. He sent Msgr. B. up to the town with instructions to start a

198

parish. The poor man took a census of the place and found about a dozen families as potential members.

Msgr. Brophy was what is called in the trade a "B.T.O." -- "Big Time Operator." He formulated a plan. A friend of his was a timber baron in Washington State. He contacted the baron and told him his plan -- a huge cross carved out of a giant redwood tree. He got it -- most likely for nothing -- set the cross up on a gentle knoll on the property and bulldozed out an amphitheater in front of the cross where Mass is said when weather permits.

Then he put signs up all over the State of Michigan informing people how close they were to "The Cross in the Woods" -- "You are 350 miles from The Cross in the Woods," "You are 175 miles from ... etc." In no time it became a big operation, visited by thousands during the warm months. It is ballyhooed as the largest wooden cross in the world carved out of one piece.

So that's where I'm going, and there are a lot of pluses in the change -- and one big minus: It won't be Victoria.

"By this
my Father is glorified,
that you bear much fruit,
and so prove to be my disciples."
– John 15:8

Epilogue

It seems appropriate to give additional report on the life and times of Father Elstan Coghill, a fellow who entered this world on August 27th, 1922, and was given the name James by his parents, Donald and Elizabeth Coghill. He was interviewed for the Gazette a few days prior to his arrival at St. Victoria. That story has been incorporated here, along with many reminiscent tidbits gathered over time – and usually over dinner conversation. For the past eleven months, from August of 1995 to July of 1996, Father Elstan has eaten most of his evening meals with this editor and her family. When the Franciscan Friary in Chaska was closed, Father needed a place for repast, and I invited him to join us. He did. It has been a remarkable time for our family, filled with the best of fun and challenging conversation, prayers before meals, and thoughtful, as well as hilarious, stories. No one tells jokes like Father Elstan. He often speaks with bowed head and, just as often, with animation – but always in humble manner and tone. Father's adoption into our family was fortuitous, for without it I wouldn't have much of this story. I did not have serious intention for PRINTS OF A PRIEST – nor this story – until well into his time with our family, and he was never made aware of such intention. I have recorded here the life of Father Elstan as I heard it, for those who love him and for those who may come to love him through this book.

***

"I'm going to put in Frieda and my toothbrush and come on over," said Father Elstan Coghill shortly before his arrival at St. Victoria. Having just spent two years at St. Hubert's in Chanhassen, the town seven miles east of his new assignment, Father Elstan became the priest in Victoria on June 19th, 1985. Frieda was Father's toy dachshund at the time. "I've had her for twelve years," he said. "I enjoy her and appreciate her."

How Frieda acquired her name hints of Father's early childhood. "When I was a little kid and my mother was having a baby every other year," he said, "we always got an old German lady to come in and help out. Her name was Frieda. She was a delightful old lady. We loved her. She always defended us kids and said we didn't do anything wrong -- but, of course, we did. So I have a German dog, a dachshund, and her name is Frieda."

When the brothers Jesse and James -- yes, the association may be appropriate -- were children, they took baths in a washtub in the middle of their kitchen floor. Father recalled the story: "After our baths one evening, I pushed Jesse back into the tub, making a big splash and mess on the floor. When Mom walked angrily in, Jesse stood up naked in the tub and said, 'You can't pin anything on me.' That cracked her up, and she couldn't carry on with any punishment." Commenting on the nature of his parents, Father has said, "My dad may have talked more, but my mother was the disciplinarian."

Father ran away from home many times as a young boy, "probably because I was in a fight with my oldest sister," he said. "Mom watched me run all the way," he added with a laugh -- admitting as an afterthought, "I think I had a problem with domination by adults."

Born in Shakopee in a six-room clinic run by Dr. Fischer, "a little potbellied family doctor," Father grew up on a farm four miles north of Jordan, a town also not far from Victoria. The Coghills, of Scottish lineage, became part of that area four generations ago. "My grandparents moved here from Canada," said Father, "and they were Episcopalians. But there were no Episcopalian churches in the area so the family attended the Catholic Church in town and converted."

The maiden name of Father's mother, who grew up in the area of Young America, Minnesota, was Smith; and her heritage was Catholic. "My mother went to school to be a nurse," said Father. "She was working at the hospital in Watertown, South Dakota, when she was hired to take care of my grandma," which explains how the Coghill factor was introduced. "My mother took care of Grandma Coghill till she died."

Donald and Elizabeth Coghill had eight children, three sons and five daughters. One of the little sons died when four days old -- at Christmas time, "a devastating blow to the family" -- and a daughter died at the age of 29 from medical problems, likewise devastating. It is James, the second oldest child, who came to be known as Father Elstan.

Formal education for James began in a little one-room schoolhouse down the way, where the total enrollment for eight grades was twenty-two. "I was the smartest kid in my grade," said Father, and he added with a chuckle, "I was the only kid in my grade. I also had to walk to school, up hill -- both ways." The young student spent more time listening to the instruction of upperclassmen than tending to his own class work. And he spent a considerable amount of time, it seems, being mischievous. In fifth grade, for example, he sent a wad of crumpled lead foil -- not the less formidable aluminum foil -- sailing across the room with the back of a girl's head as his intended target. "But I hit a boy in the back of his earlobe," said Father, "and he shot to the ceiling. It must have hurt like the dickens." Attesting to his instinct for survival, James did not 'fess up. "He was bigger than I was," explained Father. "He didn't know who did it then, and he doesn't know to this day who did it."

The next year, in sixth grade, James Coghill found himself in a more religious, and perhaps more disciplined, setting at the Catholic school in Jordan, where he entertained thoughts about becoming a priest. St. John's School however, was less responsible for these thoughts than the farm. "I hated farming!" he stated. "I couldn't see milking cows and chasing flies and mosquitoes off my head for the rest of my life. The most fun I ever had milking cows was when a cat or rooster walked in the door. We'd squeeze and aim. Some cows were better for this than others."

In spite of the fact that his father was a jockey -- he drove a surrey -- James never developed a fondness for horses. "Other people made riding horses look so simple," said Father, "but I could never impose my will on them. They wouldn't go in the direction I steered. And every time I got on a horse, my legs stuck straight out. My dad would give me an old Belgian plug to ride and they were so wide. Still my dad would say, 'I'm proud of you, son,' and try to make me feel good." Mr. Coghill is remembered in another way: "My dad sang and yodeled like Eddy Arnold," said Father, "and he looked like him, too, with the big proboscis."

Sending a son off to the seminary required sacrifice on the part of the family, especially during these years of the Great Depression. It cost them $60 semi-annually. "It would have been a lot more expensive if I'd have stayed home," surmised Father, "because I probably would have crashed a few cars or something like that" -- referring indirectly to his right foot, which is laden with lead to this day, much like his mother's, apparently. Anyhow, during the summers Father returned to the family farm in Jordan and became re-acquainted with parents, siblings, and farm work.

When it came time for James to leave home in the fall, his mother would always straighten her son's collar, "regardless of it needing straightening or not." Asked Father today, "Why do mothers always do that?" In that generation, it was, perhaps, a mother's way of touching her son and saying, "I'm proud of you. I love you and will miss you."

James chose to become a Franciscan priest, versus a Benedictine or a diocesan priest, for example, "because I didn't know there were any other kinds of priests. There were Franciscans in our parish at Jordan. And other guys I knew were becoming Franciscans. We could travel together and not get lost at

Union Station in Chicago." He attended the six years of minor seminary at Westmont. "The building is still there," said Father, "but the acreage is now a big fancy development called Oakbrook."

While in the minor seminary, James Coghill may have escaped manual labor but not discipline. "We only got eight minutes to take a shower and a cold rinse," he stated. And he worked many hours as the sacristan, a job that entailed rising at 4:30 a.m. to lay out vestments for the priests and prepare the altars for Mass. There were several Masses going on at one time because of all the professor priests. Father's early morning duties left him more tired at night than his peers and with much jockeying to find time for his studies. Why did he agree to be the sacristan? Replied Father in humble manner, "Well, they asked me, and somebody had to do it."

Also while in the minor seminary, and perhaps a premonition of things to come, Father Elstan took up writing a column for *The Gleaner*, the student newspaper. His column was entitled, "Student Prints."

As a sixth-year seminary student, James was appointed prefect, a student monitor of sorts, for seven or eight seminarians of freshmen status. "I enjoyed them tremendously," said Father. "One time they put a laxative in my coffee cup at dinner, but I found it in time -- in the bottom of the cup. I had to reprimand them, but I laughed about it back at the rectory." To this day Father Elstan seems to find comfort -- even joy -- in detecting a nature similar to that of his own.

With the six years of minor seminary under his belt, James was off to a one-year novitiate in Teutopolis, Illinois, "where everything is explained." The novitiate was followed by two years of philosophy study in Cleveland, four years of theology back at Teutopolis, and one year of postgraduate work in Quincy -- also in Illinois.

"And that was enough!" he said of his priestly preparation. James took his final vows, along with sixteen classmates, and was ordained on June 24th, 1949. Those final vows are poverty, he cannot accumulate wealth; chastity, he must remain celibate; and obedience, he must obey his Franciscan superiors. And his new name became Father Elstan. "When we entered the order," he explained, "we were to slough off all of our connections with the past, and that meant taking on a new name, too. So I sent in three different names of my choice and my mother canceled them all. One was the name of a cousin in prison; another was the name of a neighbor she didn't like -- so I took what the order gave me." Is Elstan a saint's name? "It is now," he said with a smile. "Actually, it's the name of a fifth century saint in England. He's got three lines in *Butler's Lives of the Saints*." The feast of St. Elstan is April 6th.

Father's first parish assignment was Guardian Angels Catholic Church in Chaska, a few miles from Jordan, home of his parents, and even closer to Victoria. "They usually sent you as far away as possible from your hometown," said Father Elstan, "but they must have forgotten where I lived. Today, when some fellow requests to be close to home, they usually honor it."

What do local Chaska students of that day recall about their young priest? "He smiled a lot. His face always looked like he was laughing. He was an attractive man with sandy, reddish hair. He walked at a brisk pace. He was always jiggling rosary beads in his pocket. He was one of the guys. The kids loved him. He was comfortable to be around. He'd see a group of boys playing basketball and run in and grab the ball." While at Guardian Angels Catholic School, Father was the coach for all athletics. He retains an avid interest in most sports today.

After eight years at Chaska, Father was sent to Sacred Heart Parish in St. Paul, Minnesota, for two years, where they had a "great big beautiful church and school. Then they shipped me to Memphis for a year." After Memphis, he was sent to St. Bonaventure in Columbus, Nebraska, for six years; Holy Childhood in Harbor Springs, Michigan, for six years; St. Joseph's in Bastrop, Louisiana, for six years; back to St. Mary's in Memphis, Tennessee, for three years; then Chanhassen for two years; and, finally, St. Victoria, for eleven years -- the longest he has served at any one location.

In his assignments as parish priest, Father Elstan was a builder. As assistant pastor at Chaska, he was involved in building a large gym auditorium. While stationed in Columbus, he built an addition to the school, a gymnasium, and a garage for the Sisters. In Harbor Springs, Father took it upon himself to get a new monastery built. In Bastrop he built up the educational program by hauling in an enormous horse trailer to start his pre-school program. Upon his arrival in Victoria he had an office built onto the parsonage quarters and, if retirement had not been a factor, could have -- and would have -- helped St. Victoria build a new church for the growing community. He did put steps in place for the process to begin through the purchase of property adjacent to the historical church.

His columns in *The Victoria Gazette*, and now in *PRINTS OF A PRIEST*, feature events and characters and amusements from his days on the farm, through his young priesthood, and into the present. They also tell of some of his travels, to China and the British Isles, for example. In conversation he has also mentioned driving his mother out to the Badlands of South Dakota. "I loved the Badlands," stated Father. "They were so impressive. As we walked about, Mom picked up a few rocks and put them in her pocket. I pointed out to her the sign that said 'Do not pick rocks,' and she said, 'Oh, they'll never miss them.'" His mother had not taken the vow of obedience. The son smiled.

Elizabeth Coghill died in 1981 at the age of 87. Donald Coghill died in 1944 at the age of 50 from bronchial pneumonia, an illness that could be readily assailed today with medication; son James was studying for the priesthood at the time. "My brother Jesse lives on the home place," said Father Elstan, who has three generations of nieces and nephews. The house where Father and his brother and sisters grew up is gone, however. It burned to the ground many years ago, along with his mother's earthly treasures. Those treasures included photographs of Father Elstan as a young boy, at the time of his ordination, and as a young priest. Stated Father, "Whenever I had a picture, I sent it to my mother."

So it is now the spring of 1996, and Father Elstan is leaving St. Victoria and retiring from full time parish work and a life he has loved. "I always look forward to getting up in the morning," he said very recently, and then he asked, "Can you imagine what it must be like to not enjoy your life's work?"

His life's work -- even at the age of 73 -- has remained a 24-hour on-call job. Daily Mass and daily homilies have been his routine, along with giving instructions to those preparing for baptism, confirmation, marriage, or conversion to Catholicism. He counseled those who needed the ear and heart of a priest, responded to sick calls at all hours of the day or night, consoled those who grieved upon the death of a loved one, assisted neighboring parishes for reconciliation services, distributed Holy Communion to the elderly and homebound, guided the church choirs, parish council, and other groups. He oversaw the religious education program for children at St. Victoria and taught weekly classes at the Guardian Angels school in Chaska. In addition to liturgical, sacramental, and teaching responsibilities, Father's duties have been all encompassing at St. Victoria as they included administration of the parish.

Father Elstan is an ecumenical priest, having befriended the Moravian and Lutheran pastors in Victoria, as well as non-Catholics throughout the community. He is nonjudgmental and accepting of humankind as we endeavor to live in harmony and know truth.

And now for his retirement Father Elstan is moving to Indian River, Michigan, where Franciscan Friars staff a parish and also "The Cross in the

Woods," one of Michigan's best known and loved monuments. He will be able to live in community with other Franciscans there, which partially defines membership in the religious order. There will be work for this priest of intellectual gifts and lovable ways, but on a less hectic and demanding schedule.

It is with heavy heart that St. Victoria bids farewell to Father Elstan. But we take solace in knowing he also loved us, and has asked that he be buried one day in the beautiful St. Victoria Cemetery located next to our church. We expect that day is a long way off, and St. Victoria looks forward to visits in the interim! The path to Indian River should be well traversed -- in both directions. We will miss him so much.

When Father Elstan entered the seminary sixty years ago, it may not have been with the purest of motives. He may not have seen a flash of light streaming from the heavens nor heard a godly voice booming from behind a burning bush. But God works in mysterious ways; and He used what was necessary at the time to call James Donald Coghill to the priesthood -- and keep him there. The motivation was purified, and Father Elstan became a prince of a priest.

Editor Sue